Elizabeth Missing Sewell

Impressions of Rome, Florence, and Turin

Elizabeth Missing Sewell

Impressions of Rome, Florence, and Turin

ISBN/EAN: 9783741164958

Manufactured in Europe, USA, Canada, Australia, Japa

Cover: Foto ©ninafisch / pixelio.de

Manufactured and distributed by brebook publishing software (www.brebook.com)

Elizabeth Missing Sewell

Impressions of Rome, Florence, and Turin

IMPRESSIONS

OF

ROME, FLORENCE, AND TURIN.

IMPRESSIONS

OF

ROME, FLORENCE, AND TURIN.

BY THE

AUTHOR OF "AMY HERBERT."

LONDON:
LONGMAN, GREEN, LONGMAN, AND ROBERTS.
1862.

PREFACE.

THE following reminiscences of a few months in Italy are published at the request of private friends, and for the possible amusement of such persons as may have somewhat of a personal interest in the writer.

To the public generally they can offer no information which has not already been given by other travellers.

BONCHURCH, *April 17th*, 1862.

CONTENTS.

CHAPTER I.

Paris—Louis Napoleon—Chapel of St. Ferdinand—Modern Artists—Ary Scheffer's Studio—Old Paris—Madame de Sevigné's House.. 1

CHAPTER II.

French Railway Travelling—Dijon—Palace of the Dukes of Burgundy—Churches—Scenery—Letter from Avignon 11

CHAPTER III.

Cathedral at Avignon—La Petite Providence—Marseilles—Appearance of the Town—Hôtel des Etrangers—Hôtel des Empereurs—Strangers' Cemetery 20

CHAPTER IV.

Voyage from Marseilles—Landing at Civita Vecchia—Reports about Victor Emmanuel—Railway—The Campagna—Soracte—The Alban Mount—Arrival at the Roman Railway Station—Rome—Drive from the Porta Portese—The Fountain of Trevi—The Via Sistina—Roman Houses and Furniture.. 35

CHAPTER V.

General Appearance of Rome—View from the Pincian—Bridge and Castle of St. Angelo—First View of St. Peter's—Effect produced by St. Peter's.. 50

CONTENTS.

CHAPTER VI.

Letter from Rome—A First Drive—Age of the Ruins—The Coliseum—The Spirit of Rome... 61

CHAPTER VII.

The Forum—Height of the Hills of Rome—Fragments of Temples, &c., in the Forum—Ancient Rome..................... 69

CHAPTER VIII.

The Palace of the Cæsars—The Arches of Titus, Constantine, and Drusus—Baths of Caracalla and Diocletian—Church of Santa Maria degli Angeli... 78

CHAPTER IX.

Roman Churches—St. John Lateran—Santa Maria Maggiore—S. Paolo fuori le Mura—Private Chapels—Statue of S. Bruno in Santa Maria degli Angeli—Recumbent Figure of Santa Cecilia—House of Santa Cecilia—Church of S. Clemente—S. Lorenzo—Christian Legends—S. Pietro in Montorio—S. Paolo alle tre Fontane—Mamertine Prisons... 87

CHAPTER X.

Letter on the Condition of the Roman Population—Beggars—Lotteries—Thieves—Roman Laws 105

CHAPTER XI.

Roman Catholic Ceremonies—Letter written in the Holy Week—The Miserere—The Lavanda at the Trinità dei Pellegrini—Illuminated Pork Shops 115

CHAPTER XII.

Roman Art—Vatican Sculptures—The Apollo Belvedere—Museum of the Capitol—Gibson's coloured Statues—Storey's

CONTENTS. ix

                     PAGE

Statues of Cleopatra and the Libyan Sybil—Overbeck's Studio—Hoffman's Sculptures—Vatican Gallery—Raphael's Transfiguration—Domenichino's Communion of St. Jerome—The Loggie—The Stanze—Leonardo da Vinci's Modesty and Vanity—Joanna the Second of Naples—Guido's Aurora... 134

CHAPTER XIII.

Roman Palaces—Palazzo Colonna—Palazzo Spada—Statue of Pompey—Villa Borghese—Villa Pamphili Doria—Villa Ludovisi—Villa Mellini 151

CHAPTER XIV.

Public Affairs—Pope's Illness—Political Feelings of the People—Neapolitan Royal Family—Religious Feelings amongst the People—Italian Catechism.. 162

CHAPTER XV.

Drive to Ostia—Remains of the Ancient Town—Roman Ruins—Temple at Ostia—Castel Fusano—Roman Roads—Drive across the Campagna... 177

CHAPTER XVI.

The Catacombs—Visit to the Catacombs of S. Calisto—First Impressions and Controversies—Cubicula—Sarcophagus of S. Cecilia—Paintings of Cornelius and Cyprian—Lamps—Inscriptions of Pope Damasus—Loculi near the Graves of Martyrs—Catacomb of S. Agnese—Arenariæ—Catacomb of S. Alessandro—Stamp used to Seal the Graves—Age of the Catacombs—S. Nereo e Achilleo—Effect produced by the Catacombs—Contrast with the Pantheon in Paris 184

CHAPTER XVII.

Excavations—Cæsar's Villa—Church of S. Alessandro—Church

of S. Stefano—Roman Tombs—Roman Funeral Monuments —Columbaria—Protestant Burial-ground........................ 197

CHAPTER XVIII.

Visit to Albano—Scenery—Ariccia—Gensano—Lake of Nemi —Lake of Albano—Capuchin Convent—Castel Gandolfo— Domitian's Villa—Ascent of Monte Cavo—Alba Longa— Palazzuola—Rocca di Papa—Campo di Annibale—Via Triumphalis—Summit of Monte Cavo—Temple of Jupiter— Passionist Convent—Ride to Frascati—Cicero's Villa— Tusculum—Lake Regillus—Villa Mondragone—Political Feelings 205

CHAPTER XIX.

Cause of the satisfactory Impression produced by Rome— Fountains—Lateran—Museum—Christian and Heathen Sculpture—Etruscan Museum in the Vatican—Crypt and Monuments of St. Peter's—Mosaics—Vatican Library— Barberini Library 219

CHAPTER XX.

Drive to Palestrina—Inn—Antiquities—Citadel—Hadrian's Villa—Tivoli—Villa d'Este—Cascades—Temple of Vesta— Preparations for Departure—Castellani and Saulini's Shops —Fashionable Ornaments—Visit to the Tarpeian Rock— The Medici Gardens—Villa Wolconsky—Mrs. Barrett Browning.. 231

CHAPTER XXI.

Departure from Rome—Viterbo—Radicofani Robbers—Buonconvento—Siena—Cathedral—Istituto delle belle Arti— Church of S. Agostino—St. Catharine's House—Pinturicchio's Frescoes—The Osservanza—Luca della Robbia— Country around Siena 244

CONTENTS. xi

CHAPTER XXII.

PAGE

Florence—View from Bello Sguardo—Pitti Palace—Pictures—Uffizi Gallery—Tribune—Portraits of Great Painters—Copies 253

CHAPTER XXIII.

Distinction between Florence and Rome—Appearance of Florence—View from the Ponte Carraja—The Cascine—Revolution in Florence—Political tone of the People 260

CHAPTER XXIV.

Florentine Villas — Petraja — Careggi — Fiesole — Galileo's Tower—Michael Angelo's House—Florentine Churches—Frescoes—Tabernacle in the Church of Or San Michele—Fra Angelico—Santa Croce—Chapel of the Medici in the church of S. Lorenzo—Michael Angelo's Monuments—Society of the Misericordia 266

CHAPTER XXV.

Chiesa Evangelica—Service—Sermons—Religious Belief of the Contadini—Church Reformation — Legend — Stornelli — Baron Ricasoli—Last Letter from Florence—Power's Studio—Fedi's Studio—Dupré's Statues of Cain and Abel—Cabinet of Gems in the Uffizi—Majolica and Palissy ware—Rocchi's Copies of Pictures 277

CHAPTER XXVI.

Letter dated from Pugiasta—Country Inn—Pisa—Duomo—Baptistery—Campo Santo—Noisy Hotel—Journey to Spezzia—Hotel—Croce di Malta—Shelley—View over the Bay of Spezzia—Troop of Sardinian Cavalry—Ruta—View over the Gulf of Genoa—Genoa—Tidings of Count Cavour's death—Conversation with a Sicilian Gentleman—Ratazzi—Cavour's Habits of Life—Turin—Funeral Procession—Grief of the People 294

CHAPTER XXVII.

Impression produced by Turin—Palazzo Madama—Pictures—Museum—Armory—Royal Palace—Chapel—Visit of the Sicilian Friend—Opinion of the English 308

CHAPTER XXVIII.

Drive to the Superga—Exterior of the Church—Hailstorm—View—Interior of the Church—Crypt—Monuments to the Royal Family and Inscriptions — The Custode's opinion of Cavour — Visit from a Parliamentary Deputy — Chamber of Deputies — Members — Discussion— Voting — Italian Struggle for Liberty—Field of Magenta—Venetian Travellers—State of Venice—Sorrow for Cavour's Death—Funeral Inscription at Milan—Como—Walk by the side of the Lake—Monte Bisbino—Political Feelings of a Guide—Villa Pliniana—Farewell to Italy 316

IMPRESSIONS

OF

ROME, FLORENCE, AND TURIN.

CHAPTER I.

Paris, Hôtel du Rhin, February 28*th—March* 5*th.*
—No English person thinks of describing Paris, still less of enumerating the sights. It really seems to belong to us nearly as much as London. Americans also are more at home there than they are in any other place in Europe. They make it their shopping city, and fraternize with the inhabitants at first sight, far more easily than with us, their reserved and cold-mannered cousins. Paris is in fact cosmopolitan. In speaking of it, a certain acquaintance with its external appearance is always pre-supposed; whilst in visiting it from time to time the chief interest consists in watching its change or progress. In the latter respect the improvement within a very few years is striking even to the most superficial observer. Complain of Louis

Napoleon as we may, we must still own that he has made Paris the brightest, pleasantest, most clean and comfortable capital for strangers which can be found in Europe: the wheels of its world are so well oiled that one is scarcely aware of any friction. For persons who are there only for a few days—ladies especially—shopping is one great business; seeing pictures another. Shopping is at once rendered easy by the resolution to sit by and see one's friends spend their money, and to act upon the total-abstinence principle oneself. Temperance, under such circumstances, being too often an unattainable virtue, it is better not to strive after it, and, when one goes abroad for rest and change, seeing pretty things is found more healthful than purchasing them; being quite as amusing and by no means so exciting. One piece of extravagance I must plead guilty to, that of buying a photograph of "Les Quatre Napoléons." It was the spirit of the thing which was the temptation: the knowledge of human nature which it showed,—forcing upon the people the idea of a dynasty, a succession,—which is generally allowed to be the one great object of Louis Napoleon's ambition. The first Napoleon and the Duke de Reichstadt are shadows in the background, and the present Emperor is seated in the front, with the little Prince Imperial at his knee. Every one who looks at it laughs, and says how absurd, or how amusing; but every one also goes away with an impression that somehow—though the fact has never been realized before—there have been four Napoleons; and if they have not all sat on the Imperial throne, yet they certainly ought to have done so, or will do so eventually. I think it was Daniel O'Connell who said that it mattered not that a lie was a lie, so long as it could have the start of truth. However it might be afterwards contradicted, it was sure to do its work, and the correctness of the assertion is proved by every day's experience. And if one can not only utter a lie, or that which approaches to it, but photograph it, and put it up in the shop windows, who may venture to estimate its effect?

An American gentleman who has lived a great deal in Paris, called on us while we were there, and we had a good deal of conversation about the French people, who, he said, were now unquestionably opposed to war, whether with England or any other nation. He gave me a new idea of the present French Government by suggesting that, as the Roman emperors were the representatives of the popular voice of Rome, so Louis Napoleon was the embodiment of the Republican spirit of France. The French must be governed—that they themselves acknowledge—they have not in them the elements of self-government, yet, as a nation, they are democratic, and even revolutionary. These two conflicting principles meet in a sovereign chosen by the popular voice, and clever enough to interpret the popular will;—so it is that they are satisfied. Whether this is a true interpretation of the present condition of France, I do not pretend to say; but it struck me as supplying a key to many of the enigmas in Louis Napoleon's policy,—such, for instance, as his efforts for the cause of Italian independence, at the very time when he was exercising such despotic rule in his own country.

Carrying out, as it would seem, the idea of self-exhibition as a means of impressing the people, Louis Napoleon's portraits are repeated again and again. We saw them in numbers in the long gallery of the Louvre, framed and set against the walls ready to be taken away to different places, where each will become, if not the household god of a family, at least the municipal god of a community. All this is very paternal; it assumes so entirely that the Emperor is an object of interest and affection to his people. And then he is so respectful to the past; he has so completely adopted the Bourbons as his ancestors, one could almost persuade oneself that he belongs to them. Whilst walking down the Salle des Souverains in the Louvre, lingering over Anne of Brittany's Book of "Hours," the Cuvette of St. Louis, the casket given by the Duke of Buckingham to Anne of Austria, the box turned by Louis the Sixteenth, and—more touching than aught else—the old worn slipper of Marie Antoinette, and then examining the relics of the first Napoleon, it is impossible not to feel as though the Revolution had been bridged over, and the imperial government of the present day were the collateral if not the direct descendant of the kingly government of the last century. The members of the house of Orleans appear for the moment forgotten, though doubtless both they and their friends are biding their time. It gave me a dreary feeling, after driving in the Bois de Boulogne in expectation of seeing the Emperor, to turn aside to the little chapel of St. Ferdinand, erected on the spot where the last Duke met with his fatal accident, and to be told that it is the only property which now remains to the family. "*Sic transit gloria mundi*," though so hackneyed as a saying, is very touching as a picture; and the gentle-mannered woman, dressed in mourning, who has the charge of the chapel, and told us she was a servant of the exiled princes, showed by her quiet, respectful sadness that she thoroughly understood it. The chapel itself is as hideous as modern architecture, inferior painted glass, black hangings, and French immortelles, can make it; the most interesting thing about it being a picture representing the death of the Duke, which is placed in a recess behind the altar. As a painting it is very inferior, but it describes the exact scene—the dying Duke lying in the little kitchen to which he was taken as soon as the accident occurred, whilst all his family, including Louis Philippe, are gathered round him. It has, or seems to have, the merit of truth, and as a tribute of family affection it goes at once to the heart. That was one specimen of modern painting. We were shown several others by our American friend, who insisted upon carrying us to as many exhibitions as we could concentrate into a morning which was to be devoted also to Ary Scheffer's studio. Some of the best pictures were at Goupil's, where they were taken to be engraved. One by Paul de la Roche, representing Marie Antoinette after she had heard her sentence, ought, I believe, to be greatly admired, but it was too theatrical to please me. The expression of the face was too indignant for one so crushed and resigned; and the depth of the shadows in the background, though rivalling Rembrandt, did not produce his effect. They were not necessary parts of the picture, but evidently introduced for a purpose, to heighten the gloom of the idea.

Homely interiors seemed to be the fashion. A picture by Frère, (an artist just dead,) of a mother warming her children's feet at a stove, was admirable; and another by Messonier, of an old priest and a farmer sitting at a table with fruit upon it, was quite perfect in its way. It had all the exactness and delicacy of the pre-Raphaelite school without any of its affectations. The price, we were told, was six hundred pounds.

As to Scheffer's studio, every one knows his works, and most persons think alike about them. If he had been as superior in colouring as he was in feeling, he would surely have rivalled the old masters; but even in "Monica and Augustine," perhaps the most beautiful of all his pictures, the photographs and engravings are more satisfactory than the original painting. Scheffer's early works are much warmer than his later ones. I believe at last he adopted pale tints on principle, which is all the more vexatious.

As regards feeling, his superiority is often evident. Contrast Guido's Magdalen, for instance, with his. The delineation of a handsome, rather self-conscious woman, seated in a luxurious attitude, with her dishevelled hair streaming over her uncovered neck, can by no means accord with the idea of penitence, even though her eyes may be turned up to heaven, and a skull may be resting on the table beside her. One could never be the better for looking at such a picture; whilst Scheffer's Magdalen, clinging in anguish to the Cross, is a painting which, though it may be greatly inferior to Guido's in colouring, one would desire to have continually present, as teaching more powerfully than any sermon.

There was a very striking portrait of the Abbé Lamennais in the studio, and I can imagine it to have been taken "*con amore;*" at least Mrs. Grote's life of Scheffer indicates somewhat of the same free, ardent, but by no means sound tone of mind in Scheffer, which excited my interest, and even admiration, years ago, when I read the "*Paroles d'un Croyant,*" without seeing to what they were tending, and which afterwards brought the Abbé under the sentence of Papal excommunication. Another drawing, a sketch of "The Temptation," was marvellous from the expression thrown into the countenance of Satan. He is really the fallen angel; not so powerful as Milton represents him, but almost noble in his fierce beauty. The Face of our Lord fails, as it always must. I could sometimes wish that I had never seen it attempted.

Fascinating as Paris is in its modernized aspect, one cannot help regretting the quaintnesses of past days, and the historical traces which are so rapidly being swept away. A drive which we took one morning through the old part of the city, when we visited the Halle aux Blés,—a huge stone building on the site of a palace of Catherine de Medici's,—

and the Halle Centrale, the French Covent Garden, awakened much more interest than the sight of the Rue Rivoli, magnificent though that unquestionably is. The one point, I think, which is most striking in making such a round, is the absence of all relics or memories connected with the Revolution. So far as I can remember, nothing associated with that period has indeed ever been recalled to my mind by any remark of a guide upon public buildings, monuments, squares, or streets. "*On a changé tout cela,*" seems the natural answer to every inquiry. The Revolution has been, as it were, engulphed bodily, and the people seem as anxious to blot it from their memories as they are to hide its few remains from their sight. For objects anterior to that period, on the contrary, the natural respect is felt and shown. Madame de Sevigné's house, which is now a boarding school, is exhibited to strangers with pride and interest. It is one of those places which I should like to visit alone, with the permission to sit down in the large square court surrounded by stone figures, into which one at first enters, and try to bring before me the historical persons who must so often have passed across it, whilst Madame de Sevigné herself was writing to her daughter in a little room which is now the scene of the daily ablutions of a number of young " demoiselles," who, judging from the accommodations provided for them—fifteen beds side by side in what was once Madame de Sevigné's salon—are not of a class for whom comfort and decency are deemed very requisite.

Happily, Paris is so within reach that one may hope by frequent visits to gain something more than a superficial view of it. Perhaps if it were not so brilliant as it is externally, if the streets were not so gay, the shops so attractive, and the Bois de Boulogne so pleasant for an afternoon's drive, persons would be tempted to search more deeply for its real treasures. As it is, the great temptation is to spend one's time in that which the Parisians describe by the word "*flâner*," and which I imagine means neither driving, nor walking, nor making purchases, nor paying visits, but extracting the essence from all by simply wandering about the streets doing just what circumstances and inclination suggest.

CHAPTER II.

Dijon, Hôtel de la Cloche, March 5th. — There are some essential differences between English and foreign railway travelling only to be learnt by experience. Persons take up a foreign Bradshaw with the full belief that, as there will be a choice of lines, so there will be an equal choice of hours. "By what train do you go?" is such a common question in England, on all the great railways, and if one train does not suit, it is so easy to find another which does, that it never occurs to us that in France the same question may admit but of one, or at the utmost two, replies; yet such is the case, so far at least as I can understand, for it would be presumptuous for a person who has never taken a degree in Bradshaw to make a positive assertion with regard to a study so intricate. To an unenlightened and groping mind it would certainly seem that the modern French railway system has merely superseded that of the old diligence. Two trains, for instance, start at certain hours from Paris, and go through to Marseilles. One is the express train, the other the slow train. Like the sun, these two trains never tire nor stop to rest, but proceed on their way on the despotic principle—

> "If you will not when you may,
> When you will you shall have nay."

There appears to be no choice of an earlier or a later train starting from any intermediate station. The French mind is simple and orderly in its arrangement, and the French people evidently do not understand travelling in the sense in which we look upon it. Like the angels of scholastic theology, they would willingly, if they could, go from point to point without passing through the middle. They have no sympathy with the lingering English, who like to stop and lionize the antiquities of Dijon, or inquire into the commerce of Lyons. If, therefore, you choose to give way to such weakness,—if, starting by the express train, you travel till six in the evening, and then decline going farther, you must accept the natural punishment. On the following morning, if you wish to pursue your journey in the day-time, you must accept the slow train; there is nothing else left for you. But what right have you to complain? Had you been in a hurry, you might have continued your journey by night. Since you are not in a hurry, it cannot signify to you whether you spend six hours or three on the road. Then again, on the succeeding day, the express train will certainly carry you on if you like it; but if you go by it you must take it on its own terms. It arrives, perhaps, at your resting place at five o'clock in the morning, and of course it expects that you will be ready and waiting for it. If you decline because of the early hour, it can but give, what no doubt a French railway train would give if it could, a shrug of the shoulder, and once more leave you to the mercies of the slow train. And very merciful undoubtedly the slow train is. It has a special regard for the interests of every little town; the lungs of its engine are watched as with a mother's care. It has plodded for two days and nights along the dreary way from Paris, and it will be ready for you at two in the afternoon,—you will do well to lay in a store of books, food, and patience, for you can by no means hope to reach your destination till ten at night. But again, what right have you to complain? Travelling is nothing but the means to an end—at least in France—and if you will not accept this dictum, and go with the railway Juggernaut, you must not be surprised if it should crush you.

This is a subject which is of little consequence when persons are strong and travelling only for amusement. But when you have invalids in your party who cannot be ready at five in the morning, and are afraid to risk the cold at ten at night, you may be placed in a considerable difficulty. As I said before, there may be some solution to this Bradshaw problem which we were unable to discover, but, left to our ignorance, it was frequently found that we had but a choice of evils.

At Dijon, however, we managed well, for we arrived at a respectable hour in the evening, and had sufficient time to see the town in the morning. We were as well off also at the hotel as we could expect to be in a country town; and though the chimney smoked at first, and the butter was pronounced uneatable, we conquered the former evil, and tried to be indifferent to the latter; whilst the oddness of the furniture, the brightness of the blazing logs of wood, and the deep sound of the old cathedral clock, were just so different from what we had been used to, and yet so home-like, as to give a certain tone of comfortable romance to our position. And of all the party I had the least right to murmur, for I was honoured with a splendid bedroom, with grand gilt candlesticks and mirror, the very apartment in which, according to an inscription on the walls, his Imperial Majesty Napoleon the Third had slept in the year 1856. I amused myself a little with thinking what might have been the "thick coming fancies" of the imperial mind on that celebrated occasion, but it is difficult to carry on imaginations when there is no ground on which to base them.

People often say, "Just imagine yourself to be so and so," but I never could imagine myself to be Napoleon the Third, and so after a time I descended to more natural and plebeian cogitations, and rested undisturbed by dreams either of Savoy and Nice, or of Sardinia and the Rhenish Provinces.

Dijon would well repay a much longer visit than we paid to it; it contains so many curious and interesting remains of the Dukes of Burgundy, especially the ancient palace, with the magnificent tombs of Philip le Hardi, and his son Jean sans Peur. The Princess Marguerite, Jean's wife, is placed beside him, and her white robe is covered with the daisy, which in French bears her name. The tombs are beautiful specimens of the Gothic work of the period, and the expression thrown into the countenances and figures of the mourning monks who surround Philip's tomb is such as is very rarely seen. The old hall, now the Museum, with its splendid mantelpiece—huge, massive, and ornamented—suits well with the lavish, though rough, hospitality which one has learnt to connect with the fiery Princes of Burgundy. Then there are churches to be studied, though we had only time to glance at them: Nôtre Dame, with a beautiful front, which in England we should call First Pointed; St. Michel, a specimen of the Renaissance, which, however it may be criticised, does certainly produce an effect of lightness and grace that one cannot help admiring; and the Cathedral, though that was inferior externally, and internally we were not able to examine it, as there was a funeral service going on and the church was quite full. Altogether, Dijon struck me as a very interesting place for a person historically inclined, and not less so for an artist. There would be such an opportunity for picturesque sketches in the narrow streets and pointed gables. In the country there is no very remarkable beauty. We had low hills the greater part of the way from Paris, and a curious orange and grey tint over the land from the gravel, and what I suppose was limestone, which formed the soil, but travelling before the trees were in leaf it was impossible to judge of the scenery. Late in the year it might be pretty, for it has the advantage of the river Yonne; and at Montereau, where Buffon lived, and where the tower in which he studied is still shown, there really is something like elevation in the hills. Vines also sound very picturesque, and of course in Burgundy they are carefully cultivated, but French and German vines twined upon stiff sticks are very different from the rich festoons of Lombardy; and to a person who cared for natural beauty, a drive through Kent in the hop season would be much more attractive than a journey amidst the vineyards of Burgundy.

Hôtel de l'Europe, Avignon, March 7th, 1861.

MY DEAR ——,

I am told on no account to write, but I dare say you can understand that at times I really feel a longing to say a few words to home, especially after a long railway journey, when I have been reading nearly all day. We have had three of these journeys successively. To-morrow we are to have a day's rest, and shall be able, I hope, to see something of Avignon. The *mistrale* is moaning ominously, and I rather shudder when I think of Civita Vecchia; but there is no good in forestalling evil, and it may be gone—the *mistrale* I mean—before Monday. . . . We travel in the greatest comfort,—plenty of books, and an excellent luncheon-basket; then at the end of our journey we have a *valet de place* waiting for us with a carriage, and find large rooms and blazing fires prepared for us. Last night we were at Lyons, which is a second Paris: the hotel was magnificent. To-night, at Avignon, we have quaint, large rooms, and a little Italian barbarism; tall houses and quiet streets, and the outer world like the city of the seven sleepers. This southern part of France may be very lovely in summer, but just now it is rather *triste*. The tiny villages look scared, as if every one had fled from them. Where the ladies and gentlemen of the provinces live is more than I can imagine.

We have had distant views of the Alps to-day, which have always an indescribable charm in them. L—— delights in the olives—I don't think I do; they are so grey, and I prefer colour in a landscape. Every place gives one such a different feeling! Last night at Lyons I was haunted by the recollection of the revolutionary horrors, and felt as if all the glass and gilding were a mockery. To-night, there is something rather solemn in the rambling old rooms,—very handsome in their way,—with bolts to the doors which might close a prison, and large ornamented fire-places in which half an ox might be roasted. We are all rather grave and tired, so I shall just read *Galignani* and then go to bed.

Friday Evening.—The *mistrale* is blowing less this evening, which is a comfort; and besides, they say that these winds are local. We have had a quiet, pleasant day. M—— and myself went driving about this morning to the old Palace of the Popes, and the Cathedral, and to see an Orphanage; all very interesting, and making one thankful for even the very tiny knowledge of history that one has acquired in life. Anything more dusty, and stony, and decayed than this place is, I never saw, yet one could easily get up a romance about it. Madame P—— called before dinner, and I went to her house afterwards. The street might have been a back lane in an English country town, but the suite of apartments "*au second*" was bright with gilding and velvet, as French rooms usually are. Monsieur P—— says Prince Napoleon's speech is not popular everywhere, and that the party of the priests is very strong: I think he inclines to it himself. We spoke of the possibility of the Pope's being again at Avignon. It seemed strange even to mention the idea. The Emperor is restoring the outside of the Pope's palace here; it is now a Caserne.

We go to Marseilles, according to our present plan, to-morrow at twelve. Sunday will be quiet. Monday will come the tug of war, or rather, I am afraid, the war of the elements.

Yours, &c.

CHAPTER III.

Avignon, March 8th.—Certainly there is nothing like travelling to make one feel one's ignorance, and what perhaps is more important—regret it. How one looks back to days of youth and leisure, when use might have been made of the memory as a storehouse for future occasions; and how one could preach upon the subject now to young people. But it would be in vain. It seems to be an almost immutable law that no persons shall profit by any experience except their own, and so, no doubt, the world will still hobble on with the aid of "Murray," and, finding so useful a crutch at hand, will be quite satisfied without having legs of its own. "Murray," however, did not satisfy us at Avignon, being by no means so interesting as the old Sacristain who went with us over the Cathedral, and gave us a sketch of its history, which we were all inclined to believe on the principle of the Italian proverb—
" Se non è vero è ben trovato." Instead of admitting that architects and antiquaries might be puzzled as to the date of the building, and stating that the porch might have formed part of the Temple of

Hercules—but then it might not—he asserted, with
the dogmatism so pleasant to the unlearned, that
we might look upon the west end as belonging to
the fourth century; that the Saracens had destroyed
a large portion of the edifice, and that it had been
rebuilt by Charlemagne; and one assertion being
just as probable as another, we accepted his word,
and regarded the old walls with the reverence and
admiration due both to their massiveness and their
antiquity. But as we left the age of myths, and
approached nearer to our own days, such blind
faith was not quite possible. Clear views as to the
residence of the Popes at Avignon became absolutely necessary, and how I wished then that I had
all the dates and names arranged in my memory,
instead of being obliged to turn from the monuments and hurry after my companions, begging to
be allowed a glimpse at " Murray," that I might be
quite sure as to a century, and run no risk of
accepting anti-popes for real popes, or confounding
Clement the Fifth, the first of the Avignon popes,
with Gregory the Eleventh, the last! John the
Twenty-Second did, however, retain a distinguished
place in my memory; partly, I suspect, because he
was so wicked, and being one of three rival popes,
was deposed by the Council of Constance; and
partly because I knew nothing of the twenty-one
Johns who went before him, and was not likely

therefore to make any confusion between them.
His richly carved tomb, with a splendid canopy
over it, stands in the side chapel of St. Joseph,
and a most painful mockery of human grandeur it
is. Such taste and art expended in recalling the
memory of a man whose life was unfit to be dwelt
upon! And even this outward honour has not been
secured to him. In the revolutionary atrocities
which were perpetrated at Avignon, the Cathedral was desecrated, and its treasures were carried
off. The tomb of John the Twenty-Second was
at that time opened and rifled, in the hope of discovering further riches, and now his effigy is mutilated, the niches are emptied, and the tracery of the
Gothic canopy is broken. That Papal residence at
Avignon had to me always a certain romance in it
in spite of my vague knowledge of its dates. It
was an episode in history, and the fact that the
Popes should possess a territory in France, though
dating only from the fourteenth century, served to
break up the stiffness of the strict geographical and
historical outlines of the country. Like the English
hold upon Normandy, it told of a time when the
first powers of Europe were held, as it were, in
solution, and no one could tell the form they might
eventually assume. Avignon is now such an
integral part of France that it is difficult to believe
that it was not united to it till 1791. And in the
present day there is a still greater interest attached

to the only place of exile which the Popes have ever, for any length of time, acknowledged as their seat of government. No one can tell how soon such a shelter may be required again; the rumour which said that Louis Napoleon was repairing the old palace in contemplation of some such great change might have been very foolish; but the fact of its being promulgated, made one look at the old Papal chair, now used by the archbishops, with the thought that far more improbable events had occurred than its restoration to its former dignity. "Murray" says a good deal about the associations of the old palace, which closely adjoins the Cathedral; but as he informed us also that the halls in which the conclave of cardinals once sate now "echo to the oaths of prisoners, and are subdivided and filled with soldiers' cribs and accoutrements," we contented ourselves with the outside view of the tall, white, heavy walls. There is a fine view from the terrace on which the Palace and the Cathedral stand; a still finer one, so we were told, from the Dons—a public walk on a height above; but that tremendous *mistrale*, with its accompaniment of dust, was more than we could encounter— I really think it might have upset even the carriage in which we were driving.

It was much more pleasant to descend the hill and pay a visit to "La Petite Providence," a charitable institution, the claims of which had been brought before us by the mistress of our hotel. The Roman Catholic religion never appears to such advantage as in its benevolent arrangements; probably because it ceases then to be Roman and becomes Catholic. Forty years ago La Petite Providence was founded by a Bishop of Nancy for the education of orphans; now fifty are supported for £500 a year. The children help to maintain themselves by the needlework which they undertake for persons living in the town. The Sœur who showed us over the establishment was a simple, earnest-mannered woman, with the refinement not of the world but of devotion. She led us through a number of small though well-ventilated rooms, some of them the children's bed-rooms, some their working-rooms. The children themselves were charmingly clean and bright-looking, and the tone in which the Sœur spoke to them was delightful—so kind and sympathising, without the slightest affectation or consciousness of having given herself to a work of charity. A chapel is provided for the house, and of course there were the usual externals of the religious faith in which the children were to be educated; but no one could distrust the sincerity and right intentions of the persons who had the care of them, or believe that their influence would be exercised for anything but good. The Sœur took us at last into a garden, which I think she said had been purchased for them by some lady who was interested in the institution

—La Petite Providence being, I suspect, a very favourite charity in the neighbourhood.

A drive round the outside of the ramparts and by the banks of the Rhone would have made a pleasant *finale* to our day at Avignon, but for the presence of the wind, and the thought of the Mediterranean, which not even a view of Mont Ventoux—at that season a snow mountain—could make us forget.

Hôtel des Empereurs, Marseilles, March 10, 1861. —Has any one ever been at Marseilles once without earnestly hoping that it might never be his fate to visit it again? In days of youthful ignorance and innocence I recollect having before me an indistinct picture of orange groves, cloudless skies, and calm blue waters, whenever Marseilles was mentioned. Circumstances had given it bright associations, and even the reports brought by persons who had seen it failed to disturb that childish dream of a fairy city on the shores of the Mediterranean. Alas for the realities to which in this world one is condemned to wake! There may be many more painful, but none more confusing, more dirty, bustling, and, I may almost say, repulsive, than those which awaited me at Marseilles. The town is, indeed, encircled by hills dotted with villas, and I dare say there are olives, orange groves, and vineyards, in the neighbourhood, but my own recollections are only of tolerably well-built streets and open squares, thronged with black-bearded, black-haired men, apparently the least respectable portion of the European population, and all driving, hurrying, and talking, either with an air of pressing secret business, into which you would do well not to inquire, or with the reckless search after excitement which you may be nearly sure will not be innocent. This is a very hasty impression, and perfectly open to correction, but one can only tell what strikes one's-self. I never saw a place in which I should be less willing to be left alone than Marseilles. Our personal experiences were, I must confess, not likely to give us a more favourable idea of the place. We had written to engage rooms at the "Hôtel Bristol," and expected a commissionaire to meet us at the railway station, and so far we were not disappointed. A man, bearing the usual half-respectable look of a commissionaire, accosted us as we were inquiring about our luggage, and told us he had a carriage waiting for us; and leaving the maid to superintend the packages, we placed ourselves in a wretched, shattered, straw-lined conveyance, so dirty and shabby that we did not allow ourselves to look at or think about it. On we went, rattling through the streets, and forming at every turn a less satisfactory impression of the town. Each hotel that we passed suggested the idea "How glad we are not to stop there." But we went on so far that at last we became a little anxious. What should we find at the end of our journey? We drove through an open "Place," then through a tolerably respectable street, then through another, not so respectable, leading apparently to the port. Sailors and rather ruffianly-looking men were lounging about. They stared unpleasantly as we drove by. As we came in front of a kind of public-house I was relieved to think that such a place, at least, could not be our destination. It was the "Hôtel des Etrangers," not the "Hôtel Bristol." But the carriage stopped; we were dismayed, and remonstrated. We summoned the commissionaire; but no, it was all right, all quite in accordance with our instructions. The "Hôtel Bristol" was at an end—for the time at least; —it was to be rebuilt or restored; in the meantime the owner had taken the "Hôtel des Etrangers," and everyone accepted the change. Our letters had been received, our rooms were ordered. We should be perfectly comfortable, only—would we walk upstairs?

A gentleman, no doubt, would have stormed, but we were a party of ladies. And, besides, what could we do? We had been warned, again and again, not to trust the hotels in Marseilles. We had been told

that our only hope was the Hôtel Bristol. If this
failed us, whither could we go? Silently and mourn-
fully, not owning to each other what we felt, we
followed the commissionaire into the dirty entrance,
and up the stairs. The landlady met us,—a huge,
tawdrily-dressed woman with a Creole complexion,
and sharp angry eyes, which gave the lie direct to
the volley of civil assurances that proceeded from her
lips. We were to have everything we could possibly
desire. We could choose our rooms if we did not
like those marked out for us; and there could be no
mistake, for there were letters waiting for us. That,
I think, soothed us more than anything. In the
prospect of home letters we accepted our present
evil condition as irremediable, and succumbed to the
guidance of our awe-inspiring hostess. For myself,
I will freely own, that having gone through a variety
of continental experiences on previous occasions, I
was not so entirely overcome even by the smoky
walls and dusty hangings of the "Hôtel des
Etrangers."

The rooms were indeed small, the furniture was
faded, the floors of the passages were of brick, but
for two days all this might, if one had been alone,
have been thought endurable. But there were questions of health to be considered. Good beds and good
food were indispensable, and the prospect of dinner
was anything but reassuring. It was ordered

however; our luggage was brought up-stairs, our rooms were chosen, and seating ourselves on the uninviting chairs we turned to our letters. Fresh troubles awaited us. There were no *appartements* to be had in Rome; none, at least, which would suit us. The Casa Zucchari, a palace of delight as it had been represented, and on which our affections had originally been fixed, was, we had known before, absolutely unattainable; but there were other "casas" which would have been very fascinating, only they were not to be had. One gentleman had an *appartement* which was perfect, and he was absent for a time, but he was not inclined to let it. Another—but I quite forget all the possibilities which had become impossibilities. I only know that Rome to me was far off, and the Mediterranean rolled between us, and I was quite sure that wherever I went, or whatever was arranged, my individual comfort would be the first thing provided for; and so with natural, and I hope rather excusable, selfishness, I troubled myself much more about the presence of the "Hôtel des Etrangers" than the absence of the Roman Casa.

A ray of hope gleamed upon us. There was a banker in Marseilles, a French gentleman, personally indeed a stranger, but well acquainted with some of our friends, and prepared to enter into business relations with ourselves. He could at least give us the comfort of knowing that our present domicile was not absolutely disreputable, which was the idea that forced itself upon us more and more, as we considered the locality of the Hotel, and the people who appeared to frequent it. A proposal was made that M—— should take upon herself to visit the banker, and I offered to accompany her. The commissionaire was in attendance, a carriage was called, and we drove off. As we left the Hotel I glanced at the persons waiting near the doorway, and if I had had any doubt before as to the desirableness of a change of residence, I had none then.

"Very sorry, but Monsieur R—— is gone out; can't say when he will return." This was the answer we received from the neatly dressed, thoroughly respectable individual, seated at a clerk's desk, in one of the partitions of Monsieur R——'s business apartment. Our commissionaire lingered at the door. We were obliged to talk in French, and we dismissed him, but not till most unwisely we had allowed him to hear our complaint of the Hotel. The clerk evidently knew nothing of the "Hôtel Bristol," and cared less. His head, if not his heart, was in his accounts. He allowed us to wait; he hoped Monsieur R—— would return, but he could not aid or advise us. We sat down disconsolate. It was Saturday afternoon. Monsieur R—— was likely to spend Sunday in the country. If we missed him now, we might not find him again, and we could not go back without counsel of some kind. I ventured upon a bold proposition: " Suppose we act on our own responsibility, make a tour of inspection of the other Hotels, engage apartments if we can meet with any to suit us, and then go back and say what we have done." M—— seized upon the idea with an avidity which convinced me that it was a wise one, and we made our parting civilities to the clerk, begged him to inform Monsieur R—— of our difficulty, and drove off to the " Hôtel de l'Orient." Handsome enough that was in appearance, but so very unpleasing within! And we could have no rooms, or at any rate none which would at all compensate for the trouble and expense of the change, and the fight which we were certain to have with our fierce landlady. Our hearts sank, and we recalled all that had been said of the Hotels at Marseilles. One was no better than another, and we must make up our minds to our two days of purgatory. " The Hôtel des Empereurs." We gave the order to the coachman hopelessly, but it was to be our haven of refuge. There were good sized rooms with second-rate Parisian furniture, only an ordinary amount of dust, and respectable attendants, especially civil when we informed them of our misfortunes; and having decided upon engaging a set of apartments, we enlisted their services in the rather difficult task of having our luggage removed from one Hotel to another without exciting a commotion.

The relief expressed in the countenance of our friends when we drove back to the "Etrangers," and informed them that we had a carriage waiting and comfortable rooms ready for them, was quite touching. During our absence, Josephine, the French maid, had occupied herself in making a report of her discoveries as to the persons who frequented the house, and the general anxiety was proportionably increased. It was really like arranging an escape from prison; we did not, however, feel easy until M—— and myself had paid another visit to Monsieur R——, whom we found at the door of his house, and brought back with us to the "Etrangers." The commissionaire, who had discovered our plot, and was lounging about the door when we drove off to the banker's, had already glared on us angrily and been far from civil in his manner, and worse might be expected of the landlady. Monsieur R——, however, made everything easy. He was a young Frenchman, very polite, very sympathising, most anxious to do everything in his power to help us. He summoned our Creole hostess, warned her that we had been deceived, and ordered her to send her bill to him, and the meekness with which she submitted to his dictation was exemplary.

I felt so grateful to him, and he was not only so pleasant and kind, but so business-like and sensible, that I began to think whether his French tastes might not assimilate with our English ones. It was not till he called upon us on Monday at the "Hôtel des Empereurs" that I discovered that a Frenchman never loses his individuality. We were talking of Italy and Rome, and the inducements to travel. Living at Marseilles, he was within easy distance of objects of the deepest interest, and we supposed he might have been led to visit them. But he smiled blandly, yet pityingly, upon us, and replied, "Ah, non! Quand je voyage, je vais toujours à Paris. C'est là qu'on trouve tout ce qu'on desire. Les théâtres, les promenades, le Bois de Boulogne—c'est toujours Paris!"

In contrast to Marseilles, Paris undoubtedly is Paradise; yet, as I said before, there may be many more excellences even in Marseilles than I was able to discover. We were very fairly comfortable at the "Hôtel des Empereurs," and as I was ill with a cold on the Sunday, all that I saw of the place was from a drive on Monday afternoon to the mournful and crowded strangers' cemetery, where, not having a proper date to guide me, I sought in vain for the grave of one who had died away from home and friends; and was prevented from continuing my inquiry at the Bureau in the town by finding myself obliged to pass with a young companion through such very disreputable-looking streets, that I felt it would be better to return home. Such an experience, with the howling of the wind, and the prospect of a dark night on the stormy Mediterranean, was not likely to leave me with a very unprejudiced impression of Marseilles.

CHAPTER IV.

OPINIONS upon most subjects are various, but I doubt whether all the world are not agreed in considering the description of an ordinary voyage, whether long or short, one of the most tiresome oft-told tales that can possibly be repeated. The few notes which I find in my journal will give the history of our forty hours of purgatory, in a condensed and *feeling* form, for they were written under the influence of recent impressions.

"*March* 12*th*.—On board the *Carmel*, at half-past eight in the evening—wind blowing hard—told the ship would not leave till the morning. Tolerable night in the state cabin. Left the port at six— blowing hard still—blowing all day. Very wretched —ignominiously ill—most miserable by ten at night; then had a little sleep—woke again; blowing a gale, not much alarmed, but might have been, if I had known the truth. The captain would have put into a port if there had been any port to go to; as it was, he could only drive with the gale,—so we went on till the wind suddenly lulled as we passed Elba, or some island. Reached Civita Vecchia about two —most thankful!"

And we had peculiar reasons for thankfulness, for we were spared much which others had to endure. A clever Italian man-servant, who had been in the service of my friends on a previous visit to Italy, came on board the *Carmel* as soon as we arrived, smiling with delight, kissing their hands eagerly, and showing himself both ready and willing to take all care from us. We had an official permission to land at once without having our luggage examined; we had good news from Rome, and were told that an *appartement* had been engaged for us in the Via Sistina. With so much to cheer us, we should have been more than commonly unamiable if we had not felt that Italy promised to be Elysium, and that Civita Vecchia was the entrance to it. Still, there were the enduring effects of the voyage to be overcome, and my reminiscences of Civita Vecchia are, in consequence, of a very earthly kind. A good-sized bedroom, a plentiful supply of water, and a little quiet sleep,—then dinner—the chief portion of which was left untasted—and sleep again, do not sound very paradisaical, but they were all necessary as a prelude to pleasures to come. It was quite cold, and the blazing logs of wood on the hearth gave us a sense of English comfort in our large, rather bare, *salon*. In the evening, there was the excitement of a visit from the American Consul, with the latest news from Rome. The city was in a state of expectation and preparation,—tricolored flags and ribands were all ready. Victor Emmanuel was undoubtedly to make his entrance on a certain day, (I forget which,) about a fortnight from that time!

There is scarcely anything in life the loss of which we have reason so deeply to regret as credulity. That evening at Civita Vecchia was quite a romance to me, for I believed everything that was told me, if not implicitly, at least sufficiently to set imagination at work. I felt that we had arrived precisely at the right moment; that even if there were a tumult, it was not likely to be anything dangerous; that we should see a splendid sight, and that I should return home with a store of interest for myself and my friends for years to come. Now, after the experience of two months in Rome, and four in Italy, I have learnt to believe nothing; and if I could go back to Civita Vecchia and hear the American Consul talk, I should listen to him with impatience, and long to tell him that I had not a shadow of confidence in his report. But I would not do him injustice; he believed what he said—everyone believed it. There are doubtless persons at Rome who are equally believing at this moment,—and if they are happy in their credulity, why should we wish to disturb it? The French troops are, however, a reality, and so are French fortifications.

Civita Vecchia is French now. Louis Napoleon finds it necessary to provide for the accommodation of his soldiers, and also for their security. He must therefore strengthen the walls, and enlarge the outworks; and when French money and French time are expended so usefully, we are scarcely justified in saying that the Emperor has not purchased a right to the works themselves. How the Italians bear it as they do is a marvel; but they have hope—they wait in strong faith: it is only the cynical and unimaginative English who look on questioningly, and ask whether each day that the French soldiers remain in the Roman States is not a strengthening of that possession, which is said to be nine points of the law, and which may hereafter be found to be also the tenth.

I never yet heard any one describe Civita Vecchia, and certainly I am not able to do so myself. From the moment we drove under the archway of the large rambling hotel, till we left it the next morning, our thoughts were concentrated in Rome, and so I imagine it must be with most persons. The place looked to me like a set of barracks. I have no recollection of shops, and scarcely of a street. There was a railway station; but I scarcely noticed how it was reached. Perhaps, however, that arose from the fact of our pressing anxiety lest we should be too late for the train. We had gone on all the morning in a dreaming fashion—lingering over our breakfast, taking but little thought of our bags and boxes, trusting all to Giuseppe, and only thinking how satisfactory it was to be on *terra firmâ*, and how pleasant to be journeying to Rome, when a sudden rush of the porter, the waiter, and the landlord startled us with the conviction that we had not a minute to lose. How we hurried to the chamber of the one member of our party, who being over-tired had breakfasted in her own room,—how we collected gloves, ribands, brooches, and every miscellaneous article of the toilette, and thrust them into our bags and pockets,—how mercilessly we turned and twisted about our unhappy friend, throwing her garments upon her stringless and unbuttoned, and how we bemoaned ourselves, and reproached Giuseppe, and professed to give up at once any hope of being in time—and in the midst of all the confusion, what dreary visions arose of a long day at Civita Vecchia, may very easily be imagined! And after all what was our condition? We found ourselves quietly seated in the railway carriage, with time to settle ourselves comfortably, to make every arrangement for our luggage, and to laugh at our folly in having suffered ourselves to be so frightened. That is a very common experience in continental railway travelling. English and Americans are the only people who rush through life, and delight in braving and just escaping a great annoyance. "Not a minute to lose," means ten minutes to spare in France and Italy, but it is long before one can fully comprehend and accept this fact.

And of all railways, that from Civita Vecchia to Rome would seem to be the least likely to hurry and leave you behind. It partakes of the genius of the country: by the word "country" meaning the Papal States. It is not absolutely retrograde, but its advances are made in the most careful and least exciting manner. You do not rush over the Campagna, upon which you enter immediately after leaving the fortifications; you progress soberly by the side of the Mediterranean. There is full opportunity for watching the extent of the blue waters, the curling and crisping of the waves, and the white foam, so sparkling and free. You may see a steamer in the distance which left Naples the evening before, and is now coming up to Civita Vecchia to take in passengers; and you may congratulate yourself most heartily that you are not going on board. Or you may turn to the Campagna. The very name has an untold charm. What you see is, you are informed, the most uninteresting portion of the whole tract; and certainly, if you were passing over such an extent of uncultivated land in England, you might be inclined to call it so; but how can the Roman Campagna ever be uninteresting? It stretches away like a raised map; but beneath those uneven mounds, upon which flocks of sheep and herds of dark-eyed, light-coloured buffalo-oxen are grazing, what treasures of antiquity, what ruins of houses, temples, statues, columns, lie buried! It requires faith indeed to believe it; the present has so completely obliterated the past. Only the towers of a few old fortified stone houses on the shore, recall the contests of the mediæval age. The shepherds, with their rough sheepskin coats and pointed hats; the sickly peasants who here and there lie stretched upon the green bank, are now the sole possessors of the Campagna; at least, so far as life and employment can be called possession. The land itself is the property of the great nobles of Rome; but they have no connexion with it, except through the suffering, emaciated, and scattered population who are condemned to cultivate it. There are railway stations between Civita Vecchia and Rome; but what need there is of any, is a question which it is easier for a traveller to ask than to answer. No roads are to be seen, and no villages. In the distance there may be a solitary farmhouse, surrounded by a group of stunted trees; but even this is little better than a hospital. At certain seasons of the year, if great precautions are taken, it may be occupied, and some persons doubtless do occupy it; but what their lives are, and how soon they may be brought to an end, is seen by the condition of the miserable beggars, who creep up to the carriage piteously asking for money, which it would seem they can have no means of expending.

The train rolls on, and you draw nearer to Rome. Away to the north-east, a shadowy outline is seen on the horizon; its form is undulating, its tint a pale grey, deepened with blue. There is something singularly graceful in it, as it stands apart from the long line of soft and jagged hills which so nearly approach it. You could almost say that it was conscious of beauty and individuality; and when you hear that you are looking upon the "lone Soracte," which

> "—— from out the plain
> Heaves like a long-swept wave about to break,
> And on the curl hangs pausing,"

you feel that, apart from all associations, the solitary mountain has gained a place in your memory for ever.

And those jagged hills!—there is snow on their summits, and behind the openings of the foremost ridge a glistening mass is seen, which must be very far off. They are the Sabine mountains,—and though now they may seem strange to you, recalling by their names only the days of mythical barbarism, you will ere long learn to linger with delight upon the grey tints of their stony peaks,—blending exquisitely with the rich purple shadows of their deep recesses, until in idea they have become one with Rome itself,—so softening the sternness of its past, and the desolation of its present condition, that any description, or any thought which separates the ruins from the mountains, will be felt to be an untruthfulness,—an ungrateful denial of the beauty bestowed upon the Eternal City.

But you are hurrying forward, and there are indications of a close approach to a town. Cottages are more frequent, and looking to the right, a cultivated country is seen, ascending gradually to the foot of a remarkably-shaped square-topped hill, which may lay some claim to the dignity of a mountain. On its highest elevation, a convent of the Passionists has been erected, and the form of the building can almost be distinguished. The sides of this hill sink into the Campagna, which stretches away from it like the flat sea-coast—there is no visible line of separation. The Alban Mount—for it is that which you are regarding—is, as it were, a mighty upheaving of the Campagna, and having from its elevation escaped the desolating malaria, it has gathered around its base white towns and villages, glittering amongst pines, olives, and chestnuts. Marino, Grotta Ferrata, Rocca di Papa, will all in time become familiar to you; now, you scarcely look at them, for your eye is wandering beyond the Alban Mount to the far-extending slopes rich

in beauty and cultivation, which spread away to
the east, and where you may seek for places, in
thought familiar to you from childhood—Frascati
and Tivoli. It is very difficult to understand it all.
That same Alban Mount stood looking upon the
Campagna before Rome was founded; the very
stones of Alba Longa are, so it is said by some, still
resting upon its declivity overhanging the Alban
Lake; and on the summit—Monte Cavo, as it is now
called—was the great temple of Jupiter, to which
the Roman generals directed their triumphal march
when they had gained some splendid victory. It
is so impossible to think, much more to feel all this,
as you are carried along in a railway carriage, that,
in very despair, you turn away and dwell only upon
what is visibly before you. There is nothing grand
or exciting, or in the least satisfying, in that.
Before you have had time to know that you must
be approaching Rome, you are there—at the
railway station—nothing better than a railway-
station, bustling, dusty, most matter-of-fact. Neither carriages nor porters have anything peculiar
about them; and though the Papal gendarmes strut
about with cocked hats, and a good deal of silver
upon their coats, and have fierce and surly faces,
they are not therefore so very unlike gendarmes all
over the world.

I had one great advantage myself in entering

Rome; I was placed in a carriage with a friend who had seen it before, and who did not wish to talk. If I had been called upon to express enthusiasm or admiration, I should have been greatly disturbed; for, in truth, I felt but little of either. A first view of any place, of which one has for years formed to oneself a definite picture, must necessarily be a shock, even if it does not prove a disappointment. To enter Rome by the Porta Portese on your way to the Via Sistina, is to pass by the high, bare walls of the hospital of Or San Michele, and then thread your course through a number of narrow streets, flanked by dilapidated houses, and thronged with beggars, too sickly and degraded to be picturesque, till you reach the banks of the Tiber. Looking across the river, you may then see a small building, encircled by columns, and roofed with what appear to be wooden tiles, which you are told is the Temple of Vesta. It excites no poetical feeling by its beauty, and you pass it too rapidly to summon imagination to your assistance. The Tiber is crossed by the "Ponte di quattro Capi;" you have not yet learnt that it is the old Pons Fabricius, and its name is but an amusement and a wonder. So are many of the names of the streets, but beauty and grandeur are still not to be found. Only the grand, decayed, circular building—the theatre of Marcellus—upon which you

stumble unexpectedly in the midst of some most
decayed and beggarly streets, gives you a certain
thrill—a suspicion that after all you are not going
to be disappointed, that there may be something in
Rome to awaken a new and an intense interest.
And there are glimpses of nobler and more imposing
thoroughfares as you proceed, but only glimpses—
you seem to skirt them all. In and out, through
lanes and alleys, you proceed, till suddenly—you
could almost start from your seat and entreat the
driver to pause—in a small open " Place " is an immense deep basin of clear water; behind it, rocks
and statues, Neptune, Tritons, and horses, are
mingled together in such confusion, that you cannot
attempt to distinguish them. They are backed by the
façade of a Roman Palazzo, with its columns, pilasters, and bas-reliefs; and from a central niche, and
from every projection at the side, profuse streams
gush out, pouring down the rocks in foaming lines,
till they fall glittering and dancing into the vast stone
reservoir. It is such a contrast to the dirt and poverty,
the hopeless, abject decay from which you have just
escaped, that it comes before you as a marvel of
magic. The taste which designed it may be objec-
tionable, the details may be faulty in the extreme,
but the effect is undoubted. You cannot wonder that
Roman superstition attaches a peculiar power to the
Fountain of Trevi, and bids those who are about to

depart from Rome, but would fain return to it again, drink of its charmed waters, and their wish will receive its fulfilment.

The Fountain of Trevi is but a short distance from the Via Sistina, and the Via Sistina demands but a short description. It is neither ancient nor modern, neither handsome nor decayed. It dates, as one-half of Rome appears to date, from Sixtus the Fifth; and it has some good houses in it, and some very bad. That there are no porticoes to the doorways, no steps, no ornaments, is not surprising; for who can find anything like architectural beauty in an Italian house? In England, certainly, I should have been surprised to see opposite the door of a large private dwelling a dark archway, looking like the entrance to a coal-cellar, and in which, unhappy, poverty-stricken people had gathered, watching for an opportunity to beg; but so, also, I should not, in England, have expected to ascend to my suite of rooms by a stone staircase, so dirty that one could only gather up one's dress and step carefully, and be thankful that one was near-sighted. The small door flat against the wall might have been the entrance to a closet, but the bell-handle and the tinkling bell indicated something more dignified; and there was a marble tablet inserted near, with an inscription, commemorating the fact, that Thorwaldsen, the sculptor, during his residence in Rome, inhabited the same *appartement*. That was the first little romance which awaited me. There were to be many more before I said good-bye to Rome, although they were scarcely to be found in the drawing-room, dining-room, and bed-rooms, opening from an anteroom, and communicating with each other, which were to constitute our home for the next two months. Continental rooms, and continental furniture, are all very much alike; there may be less cotton velvet in Italy than in France, the fashion of the sofas may be more cumbersome, there may be a greater medley of colour,—yellow and green may predominate over crimson,—and the beds may partake rather of the quality of straw than feathers, but these are very slight differences. It is when you look out of your window into the little garden below, that you are conscious of a change. The orange-trees, the luxuriant flowers, the little rippling fountains, tell you then that you are in Italy, even before you have caught the musical language of the servants, who are chattering and calling to each other, rejoicing in the brilliant sunshine, and perhaps more indifferent than yourself to the sharp wind which accompanies it.

There was a collection of these little gardens filling the space between the backs of the houses of the Via Sistina and the Via Gregoriana; and there were some mysterious connexion between them, and a way through an archway and a courtyard, by which persons could go privately from one street to the other. The houses also seemed to have some unknown means of communication. It was difficult to tell whether the balcony at which you were looking belonged to yourself or your neighbour.

The distinction between *meum* and *tuum* was by no means clear, especially when it dawned upon you, that persons inhabiting an *appartement* on the floor above you, reached it by some courtyard quite removed from the public entrance. All this was very perplexing and rather exciting, when eventually there came a fear of robbers, and I lay awake at night thinking of the staircase between the dining and drawing rooms, which led down into unpenetrated regions, and the little door in the wall outside our ante-room, marked " studio," but leading to I knew not what.

That, however, was an after-fear. I slept undisturbed my first night in Rome—at least, when I had become accustomed to my straw bed.

CHAPTER V.

March 15th.—St. Peter's! It would seem that every one's heart must sink at the thought of having to describe or talk of it. I used to feel quite nervous when, in Rome, any one approached the subject; it was like asking what one thought of Mont Blanc. And it was really some time before I knew what I felt, though I saw St. Peter's the very first day I was in Rome. We drove there in the afternoon, in time to hear the chanted vespers, which is the usual service on the Fridays in Lent. By that time I had begun to understand that the Rome of my imagination, and the Rome of reality, had scarcely a shadow of resemblance. We had occasion to go first over the Pincian Hill (which is quite close to the Via Sistina) to the Piazza del Popolo, the large circular " Place " below the Pincian, in which the three principal streets of modern Rome—the Babuino, the Corso, and the Rippetta—converge. This may be called the foreigners' district. In that short drive I had gained an idea of the city, which nothing that I saw afterwards tended to alter. The Pincian as it is now, dates, I believe, from Napoleon. He made the public gardens at the top, and the broad zigzag carriage drive, planted with trees and ornamented with statues, by which you descend into the Piazza del Popolo. It is all too new and handsome to accord with one's original idea of Rome; and the view from it, though extremely fine, as the view of a great city, startles one at first by its colouring. The dark, rugged-looking roofs suggest involuntarily the idea of wood, and wooden roofs are poor and mean. My eye became accustomed to them by degrees, but they never satisfied me, especially when blended with the white plastered walls of the houses,—not so much old as shabby. A great deal of this disappointment, no doubt, was the result of my own previous errors of imagination, but the errors are likely to be common to all English persons. Damp and smoke, though most unpleasant in themselves, work wonderfully in giving depth of colouring; and persons accustomed to them forget that, in a southern climate, year after year goes by, leaving scarcely any trace of the effects of weather on buildings. Decay is, under such circumstances, *unpoetised*, and it is not till one has learnt to perceive and accept the counterbalancing—and, in many cases, very superior—charms of brilliant sky and warm atmosphere, that one begins to discern the true beauty of an Italian city,—even of Rome itself.

It seems almost irreverent to criticise in this way any place which is so rich in associations, and from which such great and lasting pleasure has been derived; but I am only giving my first impressions, and certainly, when we first drove over the Pincian, my feelings were more excited, from the knowledge that I was looking down upon Rome, and that the great building with its huge dome, which I saw nearly opposite to me, was St. Peter's, than from the actual beauty of the city itself. And yet the view is most lovely, and it grew upon me daily. The descent of the Pincian forms a handsome foreground, (handsome is the only word to apply to anything so architectural,) and the eye passes over the city, with its many domes, to the trees in the Vatican gardens and the dark pines of the Villa Pamphili Doria. To the south the view is rather intercepted by buildings; but to the north rises Monte Mario, a steep hill, with the Villa Mellini on its summit, and near it the great solitary pine saved from destruction at the request of the artist, Sir George Beaumont. If Rome, seen from the Pincian, is not precisely what an English mind may have pictured it, yet it must in time be appreciated as a view which, beautiful from its extent and its associations, affords a continued and varied interest.

And so also with the streets and squares below.

Grass grows in the extreme circle of the Piazza del Popolo, and you are disappointed; but in the centre is one of those rich stone fountains, so suggestive of freshness and luxury, which in Rome meet you at every turn and make you marvel at the lavish expenditure that in days gone by provided so bountifully and so magnificently for a thirsty and weary population. The Babuino and the Ripetta are ordinary streets, such as might be seen in any foreign town, and the far-famed Corso is but little better. It is narrow; and the shops are poor, at least externally. It has more regularity and greater massiveness than the Via Sistina—it looks as though it had witnessed fiercer tumults and storms—but if it were not the Corso, it would, for a metropolis, be nothing. And so far, unquestionably, modern Rome is disappointing. But you pass on farther; turning to the right, you drive through narrow streets, or rather lanes, in which the tall houses are more striking in their decay. There is an air of briskness and business in many of them, and the peculiarities of a foreign city are a perpetual entertainment. At length you emerge from the streets, and find yourself in a more open space on the banks of the river. Very muddy indeed it is; but that is no disappointment, for the yellow Tiber has been a school—if not a household—word from youth. A bridge, ornamented with statues, crosses it. Murray says that "the figures of St. Peter and St. Paul were placed at the extremity by Clement VII., in 1530, and that, in 1688, Clement IX. built the present parapet, and added the ten angels which stand upon the piers; one of which, bearing the cross, is by Bernini, whilst the remainder are by his scholars."

This would be very interesting, if at the moment you were in search of historical or artistic information; but on a first view of the Bridge of St. Angelo you care very little for Bernini, and only think of him as a sculptor who by his exaggeration, yet evident power, produces upon you an effect similar to that of the French painter David. What you really care to look upon is the enormous circular building which rises a little to the right of the bridge, and which you recognise at once as the Castle of St. Angelo. That, at least, is what you expected—as time-worn, as heavy and imposing in its bare massiveness. And it is the fortress of St. Peter —its guardian. Now—in a few minutes—you must be in the presence of the world's wonder. And so it is;—a drive through the narrow Borgo Nuovo, leading into the shabby Piazza Rusticucci—and St. Peter's rises before you.

Whether any person could be disappointed in that first view it is impossible to decide. Certainly I was not. I was quite unprepared for the extent of the Piazza, the magnificence of the semicircular quadruple colonnade, the splendid flight of steps, and the ethereal delicacy of the tall fountains. It was, like everything else I had seen, totally different from my imagination; but I felt that imagination could not have pictured it. It was too bright, too clear—the sunshine that filled it was too brilliant—it seemed made for gala days and festivals. And I—to the shame of my ignorance, be it confessed—had always fancied St. Peter's to be somewhat of a magnified St. Paul's. The legend of childhood, that the great London church was intended to rival the great Roman church, and that in fact it did very nearly succeed in doing so, had never been thoroughly effaced from my recollection. Dirt and bustle, smoke-stained walls, and sooty statues, and a crowd of surrounding buildings, would mingle themselves with my ideal St. Peter's, and the contrast with the reality was proportionably striking. I should like to throw down some of the houses in the Piazza Rusticucci, and I am not sure whether I should grieve if a few cannon balls or explosive shells were aimed at the Vatican, which is so connected with the church, and in itself bears such a striking resemblance to a manufactory or hospital, as greatly to offend the eye; but looking only at the Colonnade and the Piazza, I doubt whether anything could be found more completely grand and satisfying. The Colonnades especially are so fine, that one can quite forgive Bernini, who designed them, the extravagance of his statues, in consideration of the merits of his architecture. Murray gives accurate statistics of the number of columns, their height and adornments; my own appreciation of them was derived from the fact that the Cardinals' carriages always drove through them (no other vehicles being permitted to enter them), and that there was sufficient room between the inner rows of columns for the passage of two carriages abreast.

The Façade is open to objection, for it is so high as on a near approach to conceal the dome, but no one at first stops to think of this. The interior is the one object of desire; and the vestibule with its magnificent arcade, terminated by the equestrian statues of Constantine and Charlemagne, is alone sufficient to overwhelm criticism with awe. I passed through that vestibule again and again;—sometimes late in the afternoon, when the huge figures had caught the sunlight, and horse and rider were one glow of golden colouring, and it always struck me with the sensation of surprise, of something never seen before. But even in the vestibule one cannot linger. A dark heavy matting, common in Italy, hangs before the great entrance, and the assistance of some one possessing muscular strength is required to put it back. That gives a moment's breathing space, and it is needed. The first view of the interior of St. Peter's makes the eyes fill with tears, and oppresses the heart with a sense of suffocation.

It is not simply admiration, or wonder, or awe—it is full satisfaction—of what nature you neither understand nor inquire. If you may only walk aside and be silent, you ask nothing more. To study the details of the building, to examine the marble of the heavy pilasters, the enormous size of the figures in the sepulchral monuments, or the richness of the gilding and mosaics, would only be a distraction. All that art and wealth have gathered for the adornment of St. Peter's, may wisely be left to a calmer moment. One earnest, resting, lingering gaze upon that central spot at the extremity of the vast nave, where the burning lamps by day as by night keep their watch around the shrine of the Apostle, and you will do well to depart. The impression made upon you in that hour can never be lost or forgotten, but neither can it ever be repeated. When next you see St. Peter's it will be with a different eye—the eye of criticism.

I did not myself see St. Peter's as I should recommend others to see it. The first time I remained there too long, but the recollection of the sensation experienced still remained. The building haunted me with the sense of a feeling which I could not analyse, and for which I had no place in my mind. It was not till I had examined and written out for my own satisfaction a description, as it were, of the impression made upon me, that I could ever dwell upon the thought of St. Peter's with anything like rest; till then I was always working at myself with the question, so perplexing when put to me by others, what did I think about it?

Perhaps the answer will help others, if only by showing them, should they disagree with me, what they do *not* think.

St. Peter's is the palace of religion, as a Gothic cathedral is its home. It is a whole, absolutely complete; one vast mass of polished marble, and gilding, and mosaics. It inspires pride and wonder rather than humility, for it is a temple which speaks more of the greatness than the littleness of man, and the feeling which it excites culminates not at the small Cross on the High Altar, but at the circle of glittering lamps burning round the tomb of the Apostle.

In a Gothic Roman-Catholic cathedral, there is, to a member of the English Church, a sense of exile, which is intensely sad. One cannot help asking why one may not publicly worship in it. It is the home of our ancestors, and we have been disinherited. But no such regret is awakened in St. Peter's. It is at once given up to a class of feelings with which as Christians we have comparatively little sympathy, though as worshippers of the one great God, the Creator of all glory and beauty, it appeals to us with an overwhelming solemnity. It seems to be the embodiment of religion apart from revelation, and there is in its perfection one most remarkable peculiarity. Like natural religion it knows no time, but is at its completion what it was at its commencement. It is said to have been the work of three centuries; but the tomb of Clement XIII., with Canova's figures of Death and the sleeping Lion, is as much an integral part of the building as the mosaic of Giotto.

A second St. Peter's no one can hope to see;—for myself I should not wish to see it. It is the work of an age, (for as it has been said, the spirit belongs to one, not to successive ages,) when religion was a subject for the intellect more than for the heart. It is the expression of the ambitious rather than the devotional element in man's nature. A saint could scarcely have imagined it; and probably nothing less than the fiery energy of Julius the Second, and the determined selfishness of Leo the Tenth's artistic tastes, could have collected the treasures of richness and beauty which have been lavished upon it. As a proof that it is less a Christian church than a temple to "the unknown God," we can imagine Christianity blotted out from Europe, as it was from France at the Revolution, and St. Peter's might remain untouched, the most magnificent edifice which human art has ever raised to the glory of the great Creator.

It is true that Michael Angelo designed St. Peter's, and that he was unquestionably Christian in spirit; but the greatness of his genius was, if one may so say, its physical power, and it is precisely this which the building expresses.

A Gothic cathedral, on the other hand, is the expression not only of strength, but of weakness. It is, in its degree, a type of the Incarnation—the blending of the human with the Divine. Therefore it is that it admits of incongruity, imperfection, even grotesqueness, without any perceptible marring of its beauty. In its every stage, taking in that transition from the heavy Norman and Romanesque, in which the principles of the Gothic style are first shadowed forth, it represents some phase of human society, and thus it partakes of the virtues and the faults of every successive period. St. Peter's belongs to all alike, and so perhaps it may be that it does not touch the heart although it excites the imagination. We feel that it has no special place for us. What man in sorrow would turn for comfort to St. Peter's? as what man in sorrow would not find some solitary corner, some hidden nook in a Gothic cathedral, where even the carved mouldings of the walls would seem to be in unison with his feelings?

CHAPTER VI.

46, Via Sistina, March 18th, 1861.

MY DEAR ――――,

Of course I must write from Rome,—it would be unnatural not to do so; but L―― has saved me the trouble of telling you all we have done, so I shall only just give you my impressions. Rome is *Rome,* as L―― says; not the Rome which I imagined,—that could not be, because no place is quite what one thinks it will be,—but not the less beautiful and interesting. It is a white Rome instead of a grey one. I think that is the chief difference between " romance and reality " which I have had to encounter. As at Venice, the decay, so far as it exists in the more modern parts, is the decay of poverty rather than of age. But old Rome, more touching and wonderful than I had ever pictured it, is *so* old, so impressive from the "wrinkles on its brow," that it sinks into one's heart with a solemnity which becomes religious in its awfulness.

Age in England is reckoned from the Conquest. We have no ideas beyond—or at least, if we have, they are very vague. The period included between that date and the present, is analogous to the three-score years and ten which are allotted to man. But when you see the ruins of Rome, you are looking upon the man who has passed his hundredth year; every line of every additional year is written on his face, and the three-score years and ten become mere youth. We drove the other day, as L―― has described, round a portion of the walls, and through the Forum, and when I came back I was *quite satisfied*. I need not say more.

Yours, &c.

That was my first drive for the sake of a drive, by the Baths of Diocletian, the Porta S. Lorenzo, Santa Maria Maggiore, and St. John Lateran, and then by the old walls—with such most lovely views of the mountains—to the Coliseum and the Forum. No wonder that I was satisfied. I had seen the most interesting part of Rome; but it took much more than that one drive to comprehend what I had looked upon.

I was obliged on another occasion to go, with a friend, and spend a morning in the Forum itself, working out, though very unsatisfactorily, the meaning and position of the ruins; and when I had done that, the only conclusion I arrived at was, that I knew nothing at all about it. As conveying a general impression, however, the first drive was most enjoyable. It gave me an idea of beauties for which I had not been in the least prepared, especially the blending of the ruins, the Campagna, and the distant mountains. The effects of colour were indescribably beautiful. The deep red tint of the ruins, softened and mellowed by time; the shadows which floated across the uneven Campagna, with its green banks and sandy hollows; the deep purple of the nearer hills, and the far-off snow on the Leonessa, which rose up between the ridges of the grey Sabine mountains, were as new and unexpected as though I had never heard of Rome and its surrounding scenery before. And the ruins themselves, when massed together in one's memory, were equally satisfying. Taken separately, I doubt if any, except the Coliseum and the columns in the Forum, would have equalled the expectation formed of them; but as a whole, they gave me a perfectly new idea of age, and a distinct and keen perception of the magnificence of the city under the emperors. That the splendour of Rome dates only from that period, is a fact which one is constantly obliged to recal to mind. As a gentleman said to me when we were one day looking at the view from Monte Mario, it is singular to think that we know more of Rome's grandeur than Cicero, Pompey, or Cæsar did.

The Coliseum, the one thing in Rome that

never yet disappointed any one, was begun by Vespasian, and completed by Domitian. The beautiful Ionic portico of eight granite columns, which is the first thing that strikes the eye in all views of the Forum, belonged to a temple of Saturn, restored by Augustus. The two sets of Corinthian columns, which in like manner stand apart commanding admiration, have also been decided to be the remains of two temples—one built by Augustus, the other erected by Domitian to Vespasian. The building generally called the Temple of Peace, which is an immense and very striking ruin, is known to have been really a Basilica begun by Maxentius. The palace of the Cæsars, the walls of which cover the Palatine Hill, and the arches of Titus, Septimius Severus, and Constantine, bear witness to their date by their names; in fact, ancient Rome, as it now exists in ruin, may be compared to what Paris would be if it were at this moment destroyed; when certainly the relics of the empire would overwhelm, if not entirely obliterate, all besides.

This is somewhat discouraging to those who live in Rome, and have learnt to look at the emperors as a modern invention, and to regard nothing with reverence which dates from a period later than the mythical kings; but to a person who has the advantage of not being sufficiently antiquarian be fastidious, the magnificence of the city, brought vividly before the mind by its ruins, is accepted as a marvellous fact, whether as belonging to an earlier or a later age. It is indeed, upon consideration, even more startling and impressive in the latter case, since the power and rule of the vast heathen empire are thus placed in immediate contact with Christianity. And no lecture, no study or argument, could ever present to the eye the meeting and the conflict of the two as vividly as it is pictured in the Coliseum. In its object, its massiveness and size, the building is at once felt to be heathen. The huge blocks of red travertine which form walls, pierced with arches, and rising to a height of 157 feet,—the area covering a space of six acres,—and the tiers of seats rising one above another, and capable, it is said, of containing 87,000 spectators,—all built and prepared for the gratification of the most savage passions of mankind, would excite an actual repulsion and horror but for the Cross which stands in the centre of the arena. Looking upon that, the Coliseum becomes sacred ground, and the gladiators are forgotten in the martyrs. Rough representations of our Lord's Passion are also placed at intervals around the arena; and at these stations, as they are called, Roman pilgrims and beggars repeat their devotions. Elsewhere, they might be associated with superstition and formality; in the Coliseum, they are accepted without a thought of controversy. In fact, the one impression left upon the mind, both when seeing the building and when thinking of it afterwards, is religious. The very sight of the natural power of heathenism forces upon one the conviction of the supernatural power of Christianity; and so perhaps it is that the Coliseum is always spoken of gently, almost tenderly. The mind lingers over its decay; and imagination dwells, not upon past scenes of cruelty, but upon the "trees which grow along the broken arches," and the flowers, marked for their profusion and variety, which spring up amongst the lichen-covered walls and green grass. And when, ascending from tier to tier, at every increasing elevation a truer idea is gained of the enormous building, instead of looking down into the arena, and searching for the exact opening from whence the fierce animals were brought forth, the impulse of feeling is to gaze out upon the view over the city—the Palace of the Cæsars, the Arches of Titus and of Constantine, the trees which gather around the English burying-ground, and the green and—in that direction—almost wooded Campagna lying at the foot of the Alban Mount. The softness of nature is in unison with the Coliseum now; in other days it would have been only an oppressive contrast.

It was at the Coliseum also that the whole history

—the meaning, if one may so say—of Rome seemed to impress itself upon me. All places have a spirit derived from their histories, and all histories have a meaning, which, though not necessarily discoverable by man, is unquestionably known to God. Rome's history, it is almost a truism to say, must have a deeper meaning than that of any other city except Jerusalem. Looking down upon it from the Coliseum, it struck me that as heathenism and Christianity had met in the building in which I was standing, so in the history of Rome had met the powers of earth and heaven, of time and eternity.

Jerusalem is especially the city of another world—its history is miraculous and Divine; and thus, in the days of old, it formed a singular and most striking contrast to the magnificent earthliness of Rome. But when the Divine element was removed, it fell, never probably to rise again, except, it may be, under some new conditions which shall restore to it the sanctity which for its sins was taken from it. From that moment the element of divinity was transferred to Rome, and but for that transference, Rome, like Jerusalem, must have crumbled to atoms. Christianity was the life-giving germ which preserved it amidst the contests of the barbarian tribes, and gave it strength to rise from the wreck of its temporal greatness with a might, which everyone must acknowledge to be nothing less than miraculous.

True, much error was eventually mingled with its exhibition of Christianity, but Romanism was not originally an ingredient of Christianity, and, therefore, not the source of its power. The new religion set forth from Rome to conquer the world before the Papal dominion was even thought of. It worked its way and transfused its principles into the nations of the West, with an energy independent of the quarrels of popes and princes; and the Christian world has ever since bowed, not to the earthly prince who holds his court at the Vatican, but to the spirit which he embodies and represents. It is not necessary to be a Roman Catholic to feel the sacredness of Rome. Let the Pope be dethroned to-morrow, yet his city must still be the centre of Christendom; for it was there that the spiritual and Divine first came in contact with the material and earthly, and triumphantly overthrew it. Heathen Rome may be awful from its wickedness, Christian Rome may be mournful from its errors, but the *spirit* of Rome must always demand our reverence, since it is nothing less than the Spirit of God's Providence working for the salvation of mankind and the interests of Eternity.

CHAPTER VII.

ONE idea, one impression, is as much as the mind can well bear when we are seeing places which possess any very great interest; the result otherwise is confusion, and consequent indifference. The Coliseum, the Forum, and the Palace of the Cæsars, stand out perfectly distinct in my imagination, because, although on the occasion of that first drive I had a cursory view of them all, yet my actual visits to each were made separately. The Forum, to a classical scholar, would no doubt be the most exciting of the three—it concentrates so many associations. My eyes were very unlearned ones, and if it were not that many persons are in a like condition of ignorance, my wish would be merely to mention it, and then leave it without comment. For the benefit of those who do not desire and would not understand classical disquisitions, I will, however, venture to say what I saw, and what little I understood. With the Forum must be included the Capitol, for the Roman Forum is, as Murray states, " an irregular, quadrilateral space at the foot of the Capitoline and the Palatine hills, raised by the accumulation of soil considerably above its ancient level."

That is to say, the building now called the Capitol, and built on the Capitoline hill, forms the limit of the Forum towards the north-west; and the ruins of the Palace of the Cæsars, on the Palatine hill, form its limit to the south-west. The remaining outline of the Forum is only marked by a line of mean houses and modern churches, which have had just sufficient reverence for antiquity to leave a wide open area, through which passes the road from the descent of the Capitol to the Arch of Titus. A great portion of this area is deep sunk from recent excavations, and inclosed within low walls, so that no one can enter without a guide, or at least a key; and the modern road, raised high above it, and thus enabling the passers-by to look down into it, divides it into two parts. In the midst of these excavations stand the Ionic and Corinthian columns which are so well known; and, indeed, all the interest of the Forum is, to an unclassical mind, concentrated there.

The first remark I would make upon the whole is, that it entirely upsets any preconceived ideas of the height of the Roman Capitol, and the size of the Roman temples. Again and again one is reminded in Rome that the modern city is built upon the ruins of the ancient one, and that the soil has accumulated many feet; but even allowing for this, it seems as though the Capitol could never have been, from its elevation, a very formidable citadel. When the remarkable height of the precipices on which so many of the mediæval castles were built is considered, the strength of position attributed to the Capitol of Rome excites wonder. There are many castles in our own towns, Lancaster for instance, and I should think Durham, (though I have never seen it,) and certainly Edinburgh, which must be on a much greater height. A pair of stout Roman horses will drag a carriage in three minutes from the road crossing the Forum to the top of the Capitoline; and though, as I before said, there are excavations in the area lower than the road, yet they are at no very great depth, and on descending into them one can touch the base of the standing columns, so that there could never have been any "lower deep" to increase the height of the hill. This observation as to the Capitoline may be extended to all the hills of Rome. When rising out of the Campagna, before Romulus began his city, they must have been very striking on account of their number and steepness; but taken apart, they would be of no importance. The Janiculum is, I think, the steepest, and it certainly does make one nervous to drive either up or down it; but this is owing in some degree to the *pavè* road, and at any rate the penance, if severe, is very short. The height of the hill from the market-place

of Bath to the Upper Crescent must, so it struck
me, be three times as great as the Janiculum,
though, perhaps, no one portion of the road would
be actually as steep. The precipitous character of
the Capitoline hill looking towards the Forum
must doubtless have formed its real strength. On
the opposite side, even allowing for the accumulation of the soil, it must have been much more accessible. Standing in the sunken area of the Forum,
you look up now to a large white unornamented
mediæval building—the back of the palace of the
Senator, built by Boniface the Ninth, at the end
of the fourteenth century. It would have no interest at all but for its base, which is composed of
enormous square blocks of tufa,—a volcanic stone
dug out in the neighbourhood of Rome. These
blocks undoubtedly formed a portion of the ancient
Capitol. There are also traces of the Doric pilasters
of the Tabularium, or Record Office, which was
built upon this basement, and the whole belongs to
the period when the Consular Government was established in Rome. Unimportant as these remains
may appear in themselves, they are really of great
interest, from the fact that there are so very few
ruins of any buildings belonging to the Republican
period. The rest of the space between the wall
of the Capitol and the modern raised road is
covered with fragments of columns and buildings;

the Ionic portico of the temple of Saturn, and the three Corinthian columns of the temple of Vespasian, being the grand objects of admiration. The marble arch of Septimius Severus, which forms a kind of entrance to this portion of the sunken area, is also extremely handsome, and interesting as all things must be which bear an unconscious testimony to human character or action. It was built by the Roman Senate and people, in honour of Severus and his sons, Caracalla and Geta. After the murder of Geta, Caracalla erased his brother's name from the triumphal arch, but the first inscription is still to be traced upon it. The remains of the ancient Rostrum stand within this sunken area, and very near the Arch of Severus; but they puzzled me much. I had an idea that the Rostrum was a kind of pulpit, and when I saw a semicircular basement of stone, upon which a small gallery might have been erected, I supposed at first that I had made a mistake, and was looking at the wrong object. I find, however, that the Chevalier Bunsen supposes the Rostrum to have been "a circular building raised on arches, with a stand or platform on the top bordered by a parapet, the access to it being by two flights of steps, one on each side." This description would certainly suit the remains of what is now called the Rostrum in the Forum.

At the extremity of the Rostrum, near the Arch

of Severus, is a conical pillar, the Umbilicus Romæ, from which all distances within the walls were measured. One is told also of a Temple of Concord and a portico called the Schola Xantha, close to which the Roman notaries had their offices; but it is difficult to make out the position of these buildings, and still more difficult to form the slightest idea of what they must have been when standing and perfect. The general impression left on the mind is that of confusion and wonder. Temples, public offices, porticoes! One imagines they must have covered acres of ground. But the eye takes in the whole of this portion of the sunken area at a glance; and a few minutes' stumbling over broken pedestals and blocks of stone, will carry a person from one extremity to the other.

And it is the same with regard to the inclosed space on the other side of the modern road. The principal objects of attention here are the solitary column, raised to the honour of the Emperor Phocas, and the Corinthian Columns, belonging to the Temple of Minerva Chalcidica, built by Augustus. As for any other ruins or sites, it is pleasant to examine the localities on the spot, but it would be hopeless to attempt to describe them. And the names assigned to the various fragments are but hypothetical; they have been altered half a dozen times before, they may be altered more than half a dozen times again. The gulf into which Marcus Curtius leaped is said to have opened near the centre of the area, but the information is received with about as much faith as the legend to which it relates. Persons who are classical and antiquarian may possibly indeed discover enough to satisfy themselves as to their own conclusions; but for all others the details of the Roman Forum must be an unintelligible maze of conjectures.

One thing, however, appears certain. After having examined what is now commonly known as "the Forum," one can have no idea of the extent of the real Forum, or the Forum Romanum as it is properly designated; it must have covered much more than the sunken area in which the ruins now lie. And there were other Forums immediately adjoining it—those of Julius Cæsar, Augustus, and Nerva;—within a short distance also was the Forum of Trajan, the remains of which are seen in the base of the numberless columns of grey granite now standing in the Piazza Trajano, and the magnificent pillar, covered with bas-reliefs, and having a spiral staircase of 184 steps in the interior, which was erected in honour of the Emperor A.D. 114. When these adjacent ruins are taken into consideration, it seems possible to form some definite and concentrated idea of what ancient Rome might have been. On first looking at the Forum, one supposes that one is looking at all there is to see; and the very fact of hearing of so many temples and public buildings crowded into such a small space awakens the suspicion that after all the metropolis of the world might not have been so very wonderful. But a little thought removes this impression. The idea conveyed to my own mind by the ruins of the Forum Romanum, and those scattered at intervals in its neighbourhood, is rather that which I received from Vienna, where all the business and influence of the city, and the finest public buildings, are collected in the old town within the walls; whilst the suburbs without—spreading to a considerable distance—form equally an integral part of the city, but are far less remarkable or important. The Forum and the adjoining neighbourhood must, so it would seem, in like manner have been the heart of Rome from its very commencement, and have retained that distinction to the last. If there was a West End, there are at least no traces of its existence. The Emperors certainly did not remove thither, for a very short walk takes one from the Forum to the Palace of the Cæsars. Whatever might have been the size of ancient Rome, we may be certain that in looking at the Forum we are looking not only at the centre of law and commerce, as in London we might look at the Courts of Westminster, or the Exchange, or the Bank, but also at the very focus of fashion and splendour; and then the mass of public buildings, of temples and columns, crowded into such a small space, seems only to mark the reverence paid to the great visible heart of the Kingdom, the Republic, and the Empire; whilst the adjacent Forums serve to show how, by degrees, business and trade gathered around it, not encroaching upon it or defacing it, but only doing honour to it as the fountain of their prosperity. The difference between Rome, and either Paris or London, may be seen from the fact, that if the two latter were laid in ruins we should be compelled to gather up their history in fragments, collecting ideas and suggestions from ruins miles apart; whilst in Rome, the whole, from the beginning to the end, might be read whilst standing on one spot, and that spot the Forum Romanum.

CHAPTER VIII.

The Palace of the Cæsars, the Baths of Domitian and Caracalla, and the triumphal arches, all of which, though distant from each other in situation, may be classed together as creating the same kind of impression on the mind, awaken feelings very different from those produced by the Forum. They are individual rather than general; they recal the magnificence of the emperors more than the power of the Roman people. It would seem as though individuality was required for all great architectural works. The Roman Republic has left no traces of its public buildings; the Roman Empire has left grand and important ones. In like manner, we—who as a government have for years been republican in principle, though monarchical in form— have been utterly unable to impress any character of grandeur or beauty upon our architecture; the attempt to express the ideas of many minds having ended in expressing nothing; whilst France, under the influence of one mind, has made its capital the admiration of Europe.

The ruins of the Palace of the Cæsars cover a space of about a mile and a half in circuit. They will be found either very interesting or very tantalising, according to the tastes of those who visit them. To a person who delights in picturesque beauty, they will be enchanting. The huge masses of wall are covered with ivy and lichens; the laurel and the ilex have taken root and sprung up amongst the arches, and by the side of the rough steps; the surface of the ground is broken up in every direction. You climb to the top of a wall and look down into what was once a vestibule or a library, but having now the green grass for its floor, and the luxuriant foliage of Italy for its ornament; and you look out beyond upon the Coliseum, the Campagna, and the mountains, till the influence of natural beauty can no longer be resisted, and you give up all search for the Baths of Livia, or the circular room in which it is quite certain, according to Murray, that Seneca did *not* bleed to death, and sit down upon the nearest wall to enjoy yourself in the repose of ignorance. There is one great satisfaction in this, that you know your object, and are certain of attaining it. The antiquarian may weary himself with his researches, and find them all unprofitable; but if a person can give up exactness, and be content with generalities, there is no spot in Rome where so much that is beautiful may be combined with so much that is historically important, as the site of the ruined Palace of the Cæsars. On the summit of the

Palatine, Romulus raised his fortifications, and there Heraclius, in the seventh century of the Christian era, is said to have held his court in a portion of the Palace of Nero. Between those two dates what a marvellous period of the world's history is contained! And how one longs to be able to recal it in detail! It may be impossible to decide which particular portion of the walls belonged to temples, baths, corridors, or chambers, but at least we know that from some of these upper balconies, the emperors must have looked down into the Circus Maximus, lying immediately underneath to the south-west. The Chariot races must have been watched by them with eager interest from the Palace, and the porticoes and seats, capable of containing 200,000 spectators, must have been embraced in a bird's-eye view. From hence also they must have surveyed the Coliseum, and seen the crowds thronging to the conflicts of the gladiators. The shouts of the people, and the groans of the victims, must have reached them, if, unwilling to be present themselves, they remained apart in their splendid dwellings.

If Caligula and Claudius thought of the magnificent aqueduct which they began and completed—from the Palace of the Cæsars they could see the tall arches crossing the Campagna. If the successors of Titus dwelt with pride on the conquest of Jerusalem, they could gaze below on the triumphal arch which commemorated it; and if Constantine remembered with awe the victory which had made him, at least in name, a Christian, and changed the religious profession of the civilized world, he could see, but a few yards from the Coliseum, the splendid monument of his victories, which, though its bas-reliefs commemorate battles, in its inscription tells of universal peace—"*Fundatori quietis. Liberatori urbis.*"

All that could contribute to the power, the splendour, and the fame of the Roman emperors was gathered around the Palace of the Cæsars, and it is this which so greatly enhances the value of its associations. The ruins are not only picturesque and important in themselves, but excite a singular interest from the circumstance that the surrounding objects so harmonise with them, and enable us to summon up the train of ideas and associations which they must probably have awakened in the minds of the emperors as well as in our own.

The Arch of Titus—erected, it is supposed, in the time of Domitian—disappointed me, though it is said to be the most beautiful of all the triumphal arches. It was smaller than I had expected, and though it is built of white marble, the discoloration of centuries prevents one at first from recognising the fact. Its great attraction lies in the bas-relief representing the procession bearing the treasures taken from Jerusalem, among which is particularly to be distinguished the seven-branched candlestick of massive gold, which, on the occasion of the battle between Maxentius and Constantine, fell from the Milvian bridge into the Tiber; and will, so I have heard it declared, certainly be recovered if ever the Roman Government should undertake to drain the Tiber.

The Arch of Constantine, though more open to criticism, is much more imposing. It consists of three archways ornamented with bas-reliefs, and it has four fluted Corinthian columns on each front. The position also is, to me, much more striking than that of the Arch of Titus, though the latter has the advantage of association, since it is erected on the highest point of what was once the Via Sacra, and is approached by some of the rough worn pavement of ancient Rome. The Arch of Constantine, on the contrary, stands on an open space in front of the Coliseum. There are trees close to it, and when you look through it you see the Via di S. Gregorio, also lined with trees on each side. We one day watched troop after troop of soldiers passing through this Arch in even line, with their bayonets glittering in a bright sunshine, and we thought, not unnaturally, of a Roman triumph. True, the soldiers were French, and it might be asked what business they had there; but in Rome one learnt to look upon the French as natural protectors. They were always civil, always orderly, and the city would have been uninhabitable if left without some military authority. There is another Arch, on the Appian Way, which always awoke my interest. It is the most ancient of all the triumphal arches, being erected by the Senate in honour of Drusus, the father of Claudius. The aqueduct, built by Caracalla for the purpose of conveying water to his baths, joins it, and the Porta San Sebastiano is seen through it. The aqueduct and the pediment of the Arch are in ruins, and the entablature of the latter is now surmounted by ivy and clustering weeds. The whole forms a most striking subject for a sketch, but the real charm lies less in the picturesque grouping of the ruins and the gateway, than in the fact that under this Arch St. Paul must have passed as he entered Rome from the Via Appia, when the Arches of Titus and Constantine had not yet been erected, and when the first palace of Nero, built before the great fire, extended beyond the present ruins on the Palatine in the direction of the Coliseum. St. Paul's first view of Rome! It is strange to be able in any way to picture it to one's self; but it must certainly have been one of great magnificence. The splendour of the buildings on the Palatine, and the wealth and majesty which centred in the Forum, must at once have struck his eye; and if any reliance can be placed on the tradition that marks the subterranean chambers under the church of Sta. Maria, in Via Latâ, in the Corso, as the house which, for two years, he inhabited, he would appear to have avoided the more central and, consequently, bustling portion of the city, and to have lodged in what would probably then have been the more open district of the Campus Martius.* But this will, of course, be always a matter for mere conjecture. I would only wish to guard against the idea which, as I have heard, once suggested itself to a young lady, who being informed that such an ancient dwelling, supposed to be St. Paul's, was in existence, replied, "Really, I am very much surprised; I could not have imagined that St. Paul could afford to live in such an expensive part of Rome as the Corso!"

The baths of Caracalla are also very near the Appian Way. They constitute the most perfect ruin in Rome, next to the Coliseum, and leave upon the mind somewhat of the same impression of vastness, but there is not the slightest Christian association with them. As in the Palace of the Cæsars, the extent of the ruined buildings is immense, occupying an area of nearly a mile in circuit. One wanders from hall to hall, marvelling what could have been the life of the people who there collected

* See Conybeare and Howson's Life of St. Paul.

together for luxury and pleasure. Sixteen thousand bathers are said to have been accommodated at the same time; and there must have been, besides the baths themselves, splendid porticoes and apartments for recreation and the enjoyment of art. Many of the most beautiful specimens of ancient sculpture were found in the Baths of Caracalla, and though all the statues and the columns have been removed, and thirteen centuries have elapsed since the building was utterly overthrown, innumerable fragments of marble still strew the ground; and the small portions which formed the mosaic pavement can be collected in as great profusion as the roses which cluster round the walls. These Baths of Caracalla are the only buildings of the kind which are perfectly accessible to inspection. The ruins of the Baths of Diocletian are still standing, at the junction of the Quirinal and Viminal Hills; but although they were capable of furnishing double the number of baths as those of Caracalla, it is impossible to gain any definite idea of them, as many portions have been converted into churches and other buildings. The central hall, with a circular vestibule, is now the church of Santa Maria degli Angeli; and this transformation was the work of Michael Angelo, who contrived to make the church in the form of a Greek cross, leaving eight massive columns of Egyptian granite, which formerly belonged to the hall, standing in their original position. The change that has taken place with respect to the other large public baths is still greater. Antiquarians may discover fragments of basements, walls, and columns, amidst modern streets, and in private houses, but for the research of the ordinary sight-seer they may be said to be lost. I am not sure myself whether I should not prefer the loss to the alteration. It always seems to me that what antiquity loses by such transmutations Christianity does not gain. It is striking, indeed, to see, as in the case of the Coliseum, the original building left, with only the Cross as the mark of conquest in the centre; but the conversion of a building which has been heathen into one which is Christian, by an actual re-arrangement of its parts, destroys the charm of both. The Baths of Caracalla are more imposing in their stately decay than the Baths of Diocletian in their modern restoration, and it may be they are more instructive. God writes His own lessons in desolate palaces and on ruined walls, and possibly a half-hour of meditation amid the overthrown Palace of the Cæsars, or the vast halls of Caracalla, may speak more to a thoughtful mind than the associations of Santa Maria degli Angeli, involving, as they do, a painful but inevitable struggle between the regret awakened by the loss of heathen grandeur, and the reverence demanded by Christian feeling.

CHAPTER IX.

THE mention of Santa Maria degli Angeli brings one naturally to speak of the churches of Rome generally. The splendour of St. Peter's throws all others into the background. There is nothing in the slightest degree to compare with it. But even if there were no St. Peter's, I must confess that I should be little inclined to bestow any great amount of admiration upon the Roman churches. There are three, St. John Lateran, Santa Maria Maggiore, and S. Paolo fuori le Mura, which are immense in size, and rich in treasures of marble, gilding and mosaics; but after enjoying the first effect produced by their vastness, the mind sinks back in disappointment. Great allowance must of course be made for individuals educated in Gothic architecture, and accustomed to associate that particular style exclusively with the expression of Christian feeling. Italian churches generally, and Roman churches especially, are to such persons little better than magnificent waifs of heathendom, seized upon and used from ignorance of anything better. Externally, each of the churches I have mentioned has a handsome façade with splendid columns; but, instead of standing alone,

they are all attached to some other building, such as
a convent, or the Lateran Palace, so that at the
side they look much more like great hospitals than
churches. Unless you see the façade, you may
pass close to them and not be in the least aware
that you are looking at a church. Internally,
you enter a splendid nave, having perhaps two
aisles on each side, separated by rows of columns,
but it is perfectly empty, and for the most part without ornament; though the roof may be rich, as in
the case of Sta. Maria Maggiore, which is gilded with
the first gold brought from America. There are no
benches or chairs to disturb the eye, but neither is
there any effect of light and shade. The square,
unpainted windows make it all clear and bright;
you feel as you walk up the aisle, paved frequently
with marble mosaic, that you are seen from the
further end of the building, and the idea of kneeling
in prayer scarcely suggests itself. Rather you could
imagine yourself in one of Caracalla's halls; and
your meditations, if you were inclined to any, would
naturally seem to be carried on whilst pacing up
and down. There is no doubt a large amount of
rich ornament in these churches taken as a whole, but
it is too concentrated to be thoroughly effective.
Standing at the end of the nave, or what we should
call the west end—though I believe the churches in
Rome do not at all profess to stand direct east and

west—the eye passes up the central aisle, till it is arrested by the high-altar with the baldacchino or canopy over it, which is in the centre of the nave, at the point of junction with the transepts. This high-altar is always extremely magnificent. In S. John Lateran, the canopy is of Gothic work, supported by four columns of granite; in Santa Maria Maggiore, it has four Corinthian columns of red porphyry, entwined with gilt bronze leaves, and surmounted by marble angels; and in S. Paolo, the columns are of white oriental alabaster. But though all this sounds extremely grand, and though the actual marble may be most costly, yet, from some absence of association, or possibly some defect in taste, I looked at them with the utmost indifference. What did really strike me in S. Paolo, was the gorgeous colouring in the transepts, and the tribune, or what we should call the apse, behind the high-altar. It is there, indeed, that in all the churches the effect of richness is seen. The vaults are almost always covered with most curious old frescoes and mosaics; the latter, in St. John Lateran, and Santa Maria Maggiore, being especially remarkable. S. Paolo is for the most part a modern church, built upon the ruins of a very handsome and very ancient one; the greater part of which was destroyed by fire in 1823. The colouring, therefore, is much brighter; the gold of the mosaics, even of those which were saved from the fire, and have since been repaired, is glittering; the frescoes in the transepts, representing the history of St. Paul, are fresh and brilliant; and the marble and malachite which have been lavished upon the east end of the building are gorgeous. There is also more colour in the nave, owing to the series of mosaic portraits of the Popes, which are in process of being placed not only in the transepts, but over the arches in all the aisles. I saw S. Paolo first under very advantageous circumstances, which may account for the effect it produced upon me being greater than that of St. John Lateran or Santa Maria Maggiore, which I believe are considered much finer buildings. I had no particular idea of what I was going to see, and when, after a short drive out of Rome, we stopped at the large barrack-like building, with only a side view of the handsome façade, and entered by the transept, just as a grand ceremonial was going on, in which an archbishop in his splendid robes officiated, I was quite dazzled by the richness of the scene which met my eye. As a *spectacle* it was perfect, though not from the effect of devotion, or kneeling crowds, for I saw neither; but the white and violet robes of the archbishop, the dresses of the priests worked in gold and colours, the fresh hues of the frescoes, the polished marble and malachite, and the rich gilding and rainbow brightness of the new mosaic work, were perfectly gorgeous; whilst the bareness of the nave was hidden, and the people who were present, being all collected in the tribune and transepts, gave—what these vast open churches generally want—a meaning and life to the building.

This church of S. Paolo is still unfinished, but however magnificent it may be when completed, it can never possess the interest of the old building, with the tomb under the high-altar, which from the earliest times had been pointed out as the burial-place of the Apostle. It must always, however, have a special interest for English persons, from the fact that, before the Reformation, the Sovereigns of England were considered its protectors; and that when the rebuilding began, this protection was so far recognised, that the question was discussed (at least so I was told) whether application for aid might not be made to the Queen. It would be very uninteresting to go through all the churches in Rome, and describe what was particularly worth seeing in each, for detailed descriptions scarcely ever give any real impression of the thing seen. They are most helpful when you are actually in presence of the object, and, in Rome, one can read a guide-book as readily as a novel; but with regard to persons at a distance, those who have beheld what is so minutely described do not need the repetition, and those who have not would be very little wiser after they had read the account than they were before. There is one church, however, which need not be described, because everyone knows what it is like, and which yet it is impossible to pass without mention—the Pantheon. Models of it must have been familiar to most of us from our childhood, and we have no doubt admitted it into our imagination as a most magnificent building; and if the great portico, with its sixteen Corinthian columns, could be removed from the wretched Piazza in which it stands, and be freed from the associations of the dirt, beggary, and petty trade of modern Rome, it could not be otherwise than most imposing. It is one of the few remains of Roman antiquity which has acquired the grim hue of an old English building. Strangers are told that " the capitals and bases of the columns are of white marble," but this is a sad misrepresentation of facts. Marble they are, and white they may have been, but at the present moment the whole portico is as solemnly black as the most reverent admirer of time-worn and weather-stained buildings could desire. In the interior, the church, which is supposed to have been a hall belonging to some public baths, is remarkable for its circular shape, and for the singul ararrangement by which light is admitted into it from an opening in the top. To say that, in consequence, the rain has for centuries fallen through, and formed a damp pool in the centre, in spite of the drain made below the pavement to carry off the water, is very destructive of all ideas of admiration. But it is a confession required by truth; and though the Pantheon is a building which dates from seven and twenty years before the Christian era, and has columns of *giallo antico* and *pavonazzetto*, and a pavement of porphyry and other marbles, and though, more than all, it is the burial-place of Raphael, it left on my mind the remembrance of a most damp, dreary church—the very last in which I should ever desire to worship.

In speaking of the churches, it would be unfair to leave unnoticed the splendour of the private chapels attached to them, in which the richest specimens of art are to be found. The misfortune is, that they add comparatively little to the general effect of the building; they are, in fact, recesses, very frequently shut in by gates and railings of iron-work, and if you wish to enter you have to summon the sacristan, and give a fee for admission, as if you were seeing a separate building. The most remarkable chapels belong to the great Roman nobles. Santa Maria Maggiore has a splendid chapel of the Borghese family; St. John Lateran, another of the

Corsini; the Torlonia chapel, in the same church, is a perfect marvel of richness, and, I may add, waste. The fitting-up of the chapel is said to have cost £65,000; and certainly, whatever else may be said of it, it suits the pretension, if not the position, of the wealthy banker who first purchased the title of count, and whose son has married the last representative of one of the decayed but ancient noble families of Rome. There is a great deal of pleasure to be derived from the examination of all these separate chapels, so long as too many are not included in the work of one day; but this is the difficulty, unless you are a resident in Rome, and have months at your disposal. Any one would be sufficient for the inspection of a single visit. Each probably contains some monument, or bas-relief, or exquisite specimen of rare marble, or some curious relic which has a history that you would wish to remember; and which, if remembered, would be really of use as an illustration of art, or a record of past events. But one object effaces the other. At the moment you believe that you have carried away separate and distinct ideas of all that is really remarkable; but when you try to recal them, you find that, even with the prompting of a guide-book, you are by no means clear in your impression. A second visit, if not a third, a fourth, or a fifth, is absolutely necessary for any person who desires to make use of that which has been seen. What would really be satisfactory would be to take some particular line of inquiry, either historical or artistic, and carry it out by searching for those objects, and those alone which referred to it. Frescoes, mosaics, pavements, the monuments of a particular period—any of these would find illustrations in almost every Church in Rome, and when mapped out and arranged, would be a treasure for after years.

One or two things naturally, however, stand out distinct from others. There is a statue of S. Bruno, by Houdon, in the church of Santa Maria degli Angeli, which I felt sure, directly I saw it, I should never forget—it is so simple and noble; it gives one so entirely the idea of a man of intense earnestness and firm purpose, and there is such devotedness and self-restraint in the whole attitude and expression. Clement the Fourteenth is reported to have said of it, that "it would speak, if the rule of the order did not prescribe silence;" and this is precisely what one feels must have been the characteristic of the man,—an impulsiveness and determination which would have broken through all obstacles, if the higher spirit of self-mastery and obedience to law had not been completely paramount.

Again, in the church of Santa Cecilia, in the

Trastevere,—a portion of the city on the right bank of the river, said to be inhabited by the descendants of the ancient Romans—there is a most exquisite recumbent statue, a model of which I perfectly longed for. It is placed under the high-altar, and represents a young girl lying in her grave clothes, —the face averted, and the limbs rather twisted,— and the tradition which seems to be generally received is, that it describes the position in which the body of Santa Cecilia was found in the catacombs after her martyrdom. The very absence of the expression usually discoverable in the features makes it the more touching. As a glance will be more overpowering than a word, so the figure of the young, graceful, helpless girl speaks more quickly to the heart than the representation of the keenest suffering. Adjoining this church of Santa Cecilia— which is curious from its antiquity, but not at all beautiful, besides being at present shabby and dirty—there is a passage leading to a dark recess, now a chapel, and said to have been part of the house in which the saint lived. Though it was difficult to put entire faith in the legend, I looked with considerable interest upon the old walls, as our guide placed his torch in different directions to show us the traces of a furnace and leaden pipes connected with a bath-room. Part of a house of ancient Rome it certainly was, and, like the house of St. Paul in the Santa Maria, in Via Latâ, it carried one back strangely to those remote days.

Another glimpse of very old Rome may be had in the Church of S. Clemente, which, tradition says, was built on the site of the house of St. Clement, the fellow-labourer of St. Paul; and which is, unquestionably, a very early church, for it is mentioned by St. Jerome as existing in his day.

From the vaulted chambers underneath the church, which have been lately opened, you look down a dark passage which formed one of the streets of the ancient city, and perhaps this, almost more than anything else, impresses upon the mind the fact that old Rome is, for the most part, buried beneath the modern city. How it became so is a question which has never yet been clearly settled; but I suspect we have not the slightest idea of the dilapidation and decay of the city during the Middle Ages, caused by the fierce internal quarrels of the Roman nobles, and the invasions of foreign enemies. Buildings once allowed to become ruinous soon form an accumulation of soil and rubbish, and this would be increased by the *débris* brought down from the hills. A gentleman living in Rome said to me, when we were speaking upon this subject, that after watching the effects of a torrent of rain in Rome at the present day, he had no difficulty in comprehending how the level of the city had been raised.

San Clemente is—like the Church of St. Ambrose at Milan—most instructive for persons who are at all interested in working out the customs of the first Christians from the architecture of their buildings. Dating, as it does, from such an early period, it must be a very fair exponent of the religious practices of those days. It has the atrium, or court, which was first used for the catechumens; and the enclosed choir, in the centre of the building, which, however, was by no means concealed, but only shut off from the rest of the church;—at the side, by a low marble wall, and at the back by a screen formed of panels of marble net-work. There are also two ambones, or pulpits, on the right and left of the choir, which are said to be, in form, like the heathen Rostra, and from one of which the Gospel was always read. Similar arrangements are to be seen in the Basilica of S. Lorenzo; and, in fact, these two churches were more interesting to me than any others in Rome. In both there are exquisite specimens of marble mosaic,—not meaning by this the mosaic pictures in the vaults of the Tribunes, or over the arches, which are more curious than beautiful, but the patterns worked out on the ambones and altar, and especially on the beautiful candelabrum in S. Clemente. The pavements of these churches, and indeed of many of the Roman churches, are remarkably handsome in themselves; but persons who, on hearing of rich mosaic floors, expect to see brilliant colours, will be greatly disappointed. The patterns are in themselves extremely good, but time has naturally left traces of its work,—the hues have faded, and the stones are worn.

These visible early Christian remains come home to the heart at once, and are well worth the most careful observation; but the traditions were to me almost valueless. S. Pietro, in Montorio, is said to have been founded by Constantine, near the spot where St. Peter was crucified. But the whole question of St. Peter's martyrdom is involved in such obscurity, that although one may not be inclined to dispute the assertion that he did suffer at Rome, one cannot therefore accept as a fact that the hole now shown in the centre of the crypt of the little church on the Janiculum, is the identical hole into which the cross was struck. The monk who showed it was careful to take out some of the earth and present it to us as a great treasure; but I am afraid my feeling was less of reverence than pain. This attempt to locate and define what God in His wisdom has thought fit to leave uncertain, is the shower-bath which the Church of Rome is perpetually pouring down upon all genuine feeling. Truth

must be the foundation of reverence. If you assert
as a fact what cannot be proved, you give a shock
to the moral sense, and the result inevitably is cold-
ness. I could feel a great deal at the thought that
St. Paul, and even St. Peter, were once actually
in Rome, and that St. Paul, at least, must have
journeyed in the same direction, looked at the same
mountains, and lived under the same sky with myself; but when I am called upon to receive details
as to his residence, or his imprisonment, my mind
naturally enters upon a process of inquiry, and in
this act all feeling is deadened.

Probabilities and possibilities appeal to the reason
differently; they have degrees, and may be accepted or refused, according to the spirit and inclination of the recipient. No revulsion of conscience
is caused by them, and the feeling which they
awaken is, so far as it goes, as true and natural as
feeling based upon imaginative facts, (such as those
introduced into the Waverley Novels,) which every
one recognises and most persons enter into.

The one tradition which I had very little difficulty in accepting, was that attached to the Church
of S. Paolo, alle tre Fontane—built, it is said, on
the spot where St. Paul was beheaded. There is,
indeed, an absurd legend of three fountains, which
sprang up where the head of the Apostle fell and
bounded again from the earth; and the marble

pillar on which he was decapitated is exhibited, in order to destroy the faith of those who visit the spot; but the tradition as to the locality rests, I believe, on a good foundation, and there is nothing in the situation to controvert it. St. Paul, it is always acknowledged, was beheaded at Rome; and it was in this direction, towards the south, that the judicial part (if one may so call it) of the ancient city, appears to have extended. The Forum, the prisons, the Emperor's palace, and the Coliseum are all in the neighbourhood; and public executions, if they did not take place within the walls, would, it seems, have been more easily carried out by taking the criminal through the gate, now called the Porta S. Paolo, but formerly the Porta Ostiensis, than by carrying him across the Tiber, or through the inferior parts of the city.

I was going to add that, as a general rule, facility of belief in any event exists in exact proportion to the non-importance attached to it; but this I suspect would have been a mistake. Some persons have a marvellous faculty of believing whatever they wish; for myself, however, I confess that I had no difficulty in admitting that the street called the Via di S. Pietro in Vincoli, might correspond with the Vicus Sceleratus, in passing through which Tullia drove her car over the dead body of her husband; but when it became a question of Christian tradition, I felt too jealous for the truth to be contented with mere assertion.

The Mamertine prisons, begun, it is believed, in the reign of Ancus Martius, afford another instance of Christian legends, which it is very difficult, if not impossible, to accept; whilst the historical records attached to them are received without doubt. The prisons are on the Capitoline Hill, and very near the Forum. A church has been built over them, and a monk exhibits them by torch-light. You go down by steps into a large chamber—the walls built of enormous masses of stone, in the style of the Etruscan architecture—cold, dark, and damp; it would seem that nothing worse than confinement in such a place could be required for the punishment of any offence, however great; but there is a circular aperture in the floor, and by this you descend into a still more dreadful dungeon,—a circular vault, rendered doubly damp by a spring of water. In this lower dungeon Jugurtha was starved to death, and Catiline's accomplices were strangled. The evidence is undoubted, and quite sufficient horror is excited to satisfy any craving for "sensation." But legendary Christian tradition has also seized upon these gloomy cells. St. Peter and St. Paul are declared to have been imprisoned in them. In the lower chamber, the pillar to which St. Peter was bound is shown, and the spring—though specially mentioned as having existed in the time of Jugurtha,—is declared to have issued forth miraculously to enable the Apostle to baptize his gaoler. Moreover, in the upper cell, a large dent in the stones is gravely pointed out by the monk, as being the impression left by St. Peter's head, when he was thrown against it by the gaoler,—I suppose before his conversion. The stone is carefully covered by an iron grating, which of course is considered a satisfactory proof of the authenticity of the story.

These legends troubled me very little, for I not only did not attempt to believe any of them, but I was perfectly sceptical as to the fact of either of the Apostles having ever been kept in the Mamertine prison. Of St. Peter we know nothing, and of St. Paul, all the evidence we have as to his second imprisonment—which is to be gathered from his second Epistle to Timothy—implies that he was in a situation in which he could see and enjoy the solace of the society of his friends, and occupy himself with books and writing,—comforts absolutely incompatible with imprisonment in the Mamertine cells. Moreover, the Roman law was not an unjust one, it did not punish without trial; and incarceration in a dungeon is punishment. It may be said that St. Paul was placed there previous to his execution, and the fact cannot be absolutely denied because there is no record relating to it. But in his Epistle to Timothy he mentions a first trial when "all men forsook him," and refers to a deliverance (whether real or metaphorical cannot, I suppose, be determined) "from the mouth of the lion;" after which, though still kept in captivity, he was allowed the comparative freedom and relief to which allusion has already been made. It is certain, therefore, that if he was placed in the Mamertine prison at all, it could only have been during the period which elapsed betwen his last trial and condemnation and the execution of the sentence; and whether such an additional punishment was likely to be inflicted by Roman law, even upon a State prisoner sentenced to die publicly, cannot but be open to very grave doubt. As regards the Apostle, the evidence to the contrary appears to me to amount to a moral certainty.

CHAPTER X.

46, *Via Sistina, April*, 1861.

My dear ——,

You would be glad, I know, to have an idea of the general condition of Rome as compared with London or Paris; but how can I possibly give it? I can tell you about the buildings because I see them, but the people are quite different, for I really do not see them,—that is, I see only external appearances, and one learns as one goes on in life to be very cautious in forming a judgment from these. I will describe what comes before me, but I must leave you to draw your own conclusions. First of all, then, I see beggars, more degraded and sickly-looking than I could portray, or you could imagine. They haunt the streets, infest the doors, and crowd round the carriages; and no wonder, for begging is a profession in Rome. The beggars pay the Government for permission to occupy certain stations. Beppo, mentioned by Andersen in " The Improvisatore," pays for his post at the top of the steps leading from the Piazza di Spagna to the Trinita dei Monti. He is as proud of his place and his gains as an industrious artisan would be of his shop and his profits.

We passed him one day as he was riding his donkey. He recognised L——, who was with me, and gave her a friendly nod, but he did not ask for anything. He had been paid already what was considered sufficient for the time L—— was likely to be in Rome, and upon that account she was admitted to the privilege of an acquaintance. An anecdote was told me the other day of a gentleman who, being in Rome for some time, hired an Italian man-servant, a very respectable and efficient person. The man only left his situation when his master left the city. Some time afterwards the gentleman returned to Rome, and in the streets he met his former servant begging. This seemed a grievous degradation, and being willing to help a deserving person, he proposed that the man should resume his place, and the agreement was made. The servant returned to his duties, and conducted himself well. But after a short experience he came to his master and said, "he was very grateful for his kindness, very comfortable in his place, but he found it was not worth his while to remain there—it was not so profitable as begging, and he should wish, therefore, to go!"

I have no reason to doubt this story; it is but on a par with what is daily before one's eyes. Certainly the people are not to blame. The miserable creatures who are brought up to beg, and when of mature age are taught, by the Government representing the Head of the Roman-Catholic Church, that beggary is a privilege so important that they must pay for it, cannot be allowed to starve because the system which they practise is worthy of execration.

The priests give them what they can, strangers give them what they will, and as a part of their business is to excite the compassion of strangers, they must of course have recourse to artifice. Passing down the Via Sistina one afternoon, I saw a most wretched object, twisted, distorted, and scarcely human, stretched upon the ground. A lady who has lived in Rome some time said to me, when I mentioned the circumstance to her,— " Oh! yes, I have seen him; he was there one day, with a priest standing by him apparently pitying him; people collected in horror, and money was given, which the priest received. The next day he was there again, and the priest with him, ready to go through the same scene!"

No doubt when these and similar stories are repeated, a retort may easily be made by a reference to the streets of London; but the question seems to me to be, not whether begging and consequent deceit exist, but whether they are fostered and patronised. I have an actual craving for the sight of an infant school. To take up the children, put them into tubs of water, and then carry them off to some clean, large room, where their poor little bodies would be guarded from disease, and their minds opened to understand the distinction between right and wrong, would be an inexpressible relief. Charitable institutions there are no doubt in Rome, and I believe a great deal of private benevolence is exercised; but all these seem spasmodic efforts, which are of no avail whilst the heavy weight of Government influence is put into the opposite balance. Besides the legitimatized beggary within the walls, there is the natural beggary caused by the climate without. The effects of malaria can scarcely be exaggerated, for its traces are to be seen on the face of every peasant one meets. The Roman fever indeed is the dread of rich and poor. There have been several fatal cases lately within our own knowledge, almost always, I own, the result of carelessness; but the amount of care which is required for safety is startling to an English person.

The lotteries are another fruitful source of demoralization to the lower orders in Rome and elsewhere; they, also, are encouraged by Government. The servants especially are ruined by them. I know a man who last year left a respectable place with nearly a hundred pounds which he had accumulated; this year it is all gone, squandered in lotteries. The stories told of the dreams, and hints, and chance-words, which are considered indications of fortunate numbers, are painfully absurd. There is a book, giving instructions as to the meaning of the omens, and the numbers attached to them, which appears to be circulated as the Bible is amongst us. I must confess though that lotteries are not peculiar to Rome; I imagine they abound everywhere in Italy;, and no doubt it will be a difficult task to get rid of them, since they are the constant food for the people's thoughts. But there is hope under Victor Emmanuel's government that any crying evil may at length be seen and remedied. I see none under the Pope's.

Robberies are plentiful. The first night I arrived I heard a discussion as to whether it was safe for a gentleman to walk a little distance in the strects alone in the evening; and Mrs. —— tells me that she has several times found herself without bread in the morning, because the baker has been robbed on his way to her house the previous evening. We have had an alarm ourselves. Giuseppe assures us that the other night, about eleven o'clock, just as he was going to bed, he heard a noise outside his room, which is at the head of the stairs, and looking out saw two men trying to fit a key into the outer door of our suite of rooms. Hearing him move, they rushed up the stairs, but came down again, and then he called out " Thieves!" and they departed. I don't pretend to say how much of this is true, for Giuseppe is an unquestionable coward, but it has put us just so much on our guard that we have persuaded our Padrona to have the street door closed every night early. We have no porter, so any one can go up the public stairs unnoticed. It was not much consolation to be told that the thieves would not have been likely to attempt getting into the rooms, but would only have stationed themselves upon the dark staircase, to seize any one who might be coming up and down. The stiletto is far too common an accompaniment of robberies in Rome, and the police are infinitely too negligent to allow of such a probability being mentioned without a shudder. It would not be pleasant to find a murdered man at one's door in the morning, as I was told an artist living in Rome did not long ago. At a dinner party one evening, we were talking of these matters, and amongst other incidents related was one of an English gentleman, who lived in the same house with an Italian nobleman, and having gone out late, found the Italian, on his return, in the greatest alarm and excitement. Two men had attacked him on the staircase, robbed, and threatened to murder him. The Italian escaped with his life, and, in an agony of terror and thankfulness, rushed into the nearest room, which happened to be the kitchen, and fell on his knees to pour out his gratitude for his preservation. The discussion which followed this story amused me excessively, it was so charmingly national. There was but little sympathy with the unhappy man, but his conduct was severely criticised, and the conclusion finally arrived at was, first, that an Englishman would not have been so frightened; and, secondly, that he would not have gone into the kitchen to say his prayers!

Whether the Italians are brave or not—which is to my mind a question not at all decided by the fact, that a man is frightened when he is stopped on a dark staircase, and has a stiletto put to his throat,—they are an extremely agreeable people to live amongst: I doubt much whether any other nation can compete with them in the charm of gracious and graceful manner. And if, under a bad government, they have developed so much that is admirable in more important points,—what may they not become under a good one? They cheat certainly, and the lower orders tell lies to any extent. But without in the least extenuating the guilt of falsehood, I really believe that with the majority of the poorer classes in Italy the offence may be numbered amongst sins of ignorance, whilst the cheating is part of the system of trade. The generality of the shopkeepers do not in the least expect you to give what they ask; and if you do, and then complain of your loss, the fault is your own. Of course such a system is utterly demoralizing; but it is unhappily ingrained in the country, and will require years to uproot. The owners of houses and the servants will also cheat at every opportunity; but this again seems an evil inseparable from a place which thrives only upon visitors, who must have money to spend or they would not be able to come so far, and who are therefore looked upon as lawful prey. There is little dishonesty in the way of domestic stealing in Rome. Your money and your ornaments are quite safe, and as regards your bills, it seems to be considered a kind of fair game between the two parties;—one striving to pay the least, and the other to gain the most possible. And surely this, however evil in itself, is not peculiar to Rome.

There are laws here, however, which are very remarkable. One has no right to call them unfair—they would not be so if they were understood—but as very often they are not, they cause no slight vexation. I must give you one or two instances. A friend of ours came to Rome and hired a man-servant who had been living with one of the foreign consuls. After a short time she received a citation calling upon her to withhold from the servant's wages a certain sum every month,—which was to be paid to a Roman duke, whose service the man had left, owing 9 scudi. The Consul before named was applied to for advice as to what was to be done, and his recommendation was to take no notice, and the affair would die out. A similar summons, he said, had been sent to himself when the man lived with him, but he had not troubled himself to answer it. He forgot, however, to add, that his office freed him from all liability to prosecution. Our friend followed the counsel given. A second and a third citation were sent, and allowed to pass unheeded. After some weeks my friend, to her amazement, was officially informed that the question had been tried, that judgment had been given against her, and that she was condemned to pay 40 scudi; —9 being the original debt, and the remainder the cost of the suit. Being indignant at this seeming injustice, she was persuaded to try the case over again, and the result was that she was called upon to pay 80 scudi instead of 40,—and there the affair ended.

This is by no means a solitary instance of the results of ignorance of Roman law. I heard of another case, in which a coachman had run up a debt at an eating-house. Application for payment, from his wages, was made to the family with whom he lived. The claim, not being understood, was refused, and the event was they had to pay £75. But worse than all is an affair which has come within my own knowledge. Some friends of ours took a house, and when they left it it was found that some slight injury had been done to a picture belonging to the owner. A demand for £3 was made in consequence, and being considered very exorbitant it was refused. Soon after it mounted up to £7, and so it went on, till at length it had actually reached £400,—and our friends were obliged to leave Rome privately to escape the payment. This is a long letter, which I am afraid will not tell you much that you did not know before, but I can only attempt to give outside views.—Yours, &c., &c.

P.S.—As an example of the Italian perception of truth a gentleman told me that he had a man-servant who was originally a soldier in the Piedmontese army, (I think,) but had managed to leave it, and enter domestic service, though with the fear of being at any moment recalled. He came one day, and said he had a favour to ask: "Would his master be so very kind as to sign a certificate of his being very ill?" The gentleman looked at him in surprise and pain. "Certainly he would do what was required,—but he was extremely grieved,—he had not the slightest idea of such a state of things,—what was the matter?"

The man's face showed his amusement, as he quietly answered: "Oh, nothing was the matter; he had no illness, only he wished for the certificate in order that he might not be obliged to go back to the army!"

CHAPTER XI.

It is not an uncommon idea that the ceremonies of the Roman Catholic Church, as exhibited especially at Rome, are extremely impressive. There have been instances of persons on whom they have had such an effect, as greatly to tend to the confirmation of their belief in the religious system of which they form a part. With myself it was precisely the reverse. The ceremonies which I witnessed at Rome not only failed to produce the slightest effect upon me, but they appeared to me a show, and that by no means a reverent one. How far the people are touched by them I cannot say, because in the few instances in which I was present at Roman-Catholic services the poor were scarcely to be seen. The first day that I went to St. Peter's and heard the chanted vespers, the service was carried on in a side chapel. We were stationed in a little gallery, reached by some turret steps, which had formed part of the old Basilica of St. Peter. From this position we looked across the chapel to the orchestra, in an opposite gallery, and had besides a full view of the congregation and the priests below. The singers were like any other singers; they came forward and performed their parts, and retired, and made way for others; and sometimes they joined with the priests below, and sometimes the priests chanted alone; but for any appearance of devotion— to a stranger, not understanding what was going on—there was none. A moderate-sized congregation had collected about the entrance, and here and there I saw a stray person kneeling, but the majority were sitting on benches or standing; and the impression made upon my mind was that of a concert performed for the gratification of the English and Americans who chose to listen to it.

The dresses of the priests are often considered very striking, and on particular occasions they no doubt are so, from the bright colours and the gold worked upon them. But there is nothing particularly devotional in brilliant hues. They conduce to an effect; but that effect is not necessarily religious; indeed, I am inclined to doubt whether the very idea of religious *effect* is not altogether a mistake,—that is, if by religion we mean devotion. Such religion has its seat in the heart, and will therefore express itself spontaneously, according to the impulse of the heart. It is a *feeling;*—we cannot prepare for it, yet without it there can be no religious effect. This may perhaps be the clue to much which disturbs and distresses really earnest minds when they find themselves cold and criticising where they imagine they ought to be awe-struck. The very sight of a "got up" procession, and gorgeous dresses, deadens the idea of spontaneity, and the whole thing becomes an unreality, all the more painful because the feeling which it is meant to represent is in itself so intensely solemn and true. There is a good deal to be said no doubt on the other side of the question; but it would take too long to discuss it; only I think that *effect* is a word which may be applied to royal and military shows, but can have no connexion with religious devotion. There is an earthly greatness in the ceremony of a coronation quite apart from the appearance, or the character of the individual who is crowned; and the splendour of processions and dresses fitly expresses the abstract idea of kingly dignity. So also there is a greatness in the physical force of armies—apart from the purposes for which they are employed—and war-horses and their trappings, flashing swords, glittering helmets, and brilliant uniforms, represent to us the abstract idea, and therefore impress us. But there is no abstract idea of religion; if the feeling does not exist in the heart of the worshipper, there can be no religion at all, and there is therefore no power of representing it by ceremonies, apart from the concurrence of the individuals who take part in them. I felt this very much during the Holy Week. Rome at that time presented one of the most exciting, yet painful scenes I ever witnessed. With deep gratitude I would own that we had great help ourselves in the constant and most reverent services of the English Church; but when, after the hour spent there, we drove through the crowded streets to the Piazza of St. Peter's, the impression produced upon me was perfectly jarring. Rome was a maze of splendid carriages, mounted police, Swiss guards in their motley but handsome uniforms, the Pope's Guardia Nobile, and foreigners in search of penitential dissipation. The uppermost wish with every person one spoke to seemed indeed to be to get through as much religious sight-seeing as could possibly be condensed into the usual waking hours. My own heart failed me in the effort, and I saw little compared with others. The Miserere at the Sistine Chapel on the Wednesday was my first experience of the kind, and it was quite enough to convince me that I should consult my own feelings most by being contented with what I could see quietly, without rushing or crowding.

Part of a letter, written during that week, will perhaps be better than any lengthened account of what we did or saw. It is certainly likely to be more vivid than any after recollections.

Rome, Wednesday in Holy Week, 1861.

MY DEAR ——,

I hope you will all have had a letter from M—— before you receive this, telling you the details of our visit to the Catacombs and the Mamertine prisons, which we visited yesterday. To-day, after going to morning service at the English church, I did— what I wish never to do again on Wednesday in the Holy Week, but what I am very glad to have done once,—I came home and dressed myself in black silk, and a black veil, and prepared to go to the Sistine Chapel to hear the Miserere chanted by the Pope's choir. We were at the foot of the grand staircase for upwards of an hour and a half before we were allowed to go up; and when we did move, there was such a tremendous rush, as it is quite impossible to imagine unless you have experienced it. It was like being borne along by a mighty wave. I managed to get free from it for a few moments, and ran as fast as I could up the stairs, followed by M——. But then came another trial. The Pope's Swiss guards, who had been endeavouring from the commencement to keep back the crowd, were stationed at the foot of a second staircase to take the tickets, and were resolved to let no one pass without a ticket; but the whole thing was so badly managed that no one knew, or at least I certainly did not, that my ticket was required. I only saw M——, from whom I was in a degree separated, looking as white as a sheet, and trying to press forward, whilst one of the Swiss guards put his strong hand upon me and pushed me back, and the crowd pressed upon me from behind. I felt perfectly powerless, and considerably frightened, and I know I called out in English "if I might only be allowed to go back!" but that was impossible, and I was becoming quite bewildered with fright, when a Bishop, who was coming down the stairs, saw that something was amiss, and hearing Josephine, who was with us, exclaim that I was not well, and that the soldiers were behaving badly, he ordered the man to let me go on, and I was helped up the stairs by Josephine and Giuseppe. I cannot even now tell why there should have been such a difficulty. It was a perfect fight between the crowd and the soldiers. When once in the chapel I soon recovered, but I do not feel that I would go through any such experience again even for the Miserere. Putting aside the fright, it was so very disturbing, it was almost impossible to feel afterwards that one was at a sacred service. Then the crowd of chattering women in the chapel was very trying, and the long chanted psalms, which being in Latin I could not follow, tired me before the Miserere began. The Pope came into the chapel just before the commencement of the latter—I saw him indistinctly. The Neapolitan royal family were also in a raised gallery, but I could not see their faces. The Miserere itself is the most exquisitely sorrowful thing that can be imagined. It is really the wail of a broken heart, and if it could only be heard under different circumstances might be unutterably touching. We were thoroughly wearied when we reached home.

Thursday.—To-day I have been to church twice, and have seen the Pope bless the people from the balcony of St. Peter's. The crowd was not great, and only a few people comparatively knelt. The Pope was brought forward on men's shoulders (I believe, but I only saw his head), two great fans of white feathers, tipped with peacock's feathers, were behind him. There were a good many bishops and priests in the balcony with him. I don't think being *carried* is dignified for a man; but that may be my prejudice. If the crowd had been impressed I think I might have been, but the Pope's influence is so evidently on the wane that one cannot but have a painful sense of the scene being a mere pageant. The *spectacle* was splendid in one respect, from the number of magnificent carriages in the Piazza, and the gorgeously dressed Papal troops, who seem to atone in splendour for what they want in power;

but the very sight of the bayonets is jarring, when one thinks of the Pope as a Christian Bishop.

After the afternoon service we went to another sight, which came home to me almost more than anything I have seen in Rome—certainly more than any of those magnificent ceremonies—the illumination of what is called the Pauline chapel in the Pope's palace. There was an altar, looking one mass of burnished gold, and before it burned a vast number of tall candles. The only symbol on it was that, so common in early Christian times— the Lamb with the banner. Two priests in scarlet robes knelt before the altar in silent prayer, and quite motionless. The whole of the chapel was illuminated splendidly, though in a lesser degree than the altar. Men, women, and children, priests and beggars, came in one after the other, and knelt down to pray, all silently; and really, for once since I have been in Rome, I felt sad that the service and the chapel were not for us English—as well as Roman—Catholics. There was nothing jarring or offensive, only the awfully dazzling outward expression of adoration. I came home after that, and did not want to see anything more.

Easter Even.—The days are so thickly crowded with things done and seen that I despair of telling for all. Yesterday seemed as if it would be, as it ought to be, a quiet day; and so it was at first, for we were at church twice, and then went to St. Peter's to hear some lovely music. But in the evening I was hurried off into the very centre of Rome, to the hospital of the Trinità dei Pellegrini, to see a number of noble Roman ladies, in black dresses, and scarlet aprons, and crinolines, washing the feet of some of the dirtiest and most repulsive beggars that even the Roman States can furnish. They were pilgrims, come from a distance of sixty miles; and a third part of the Roman world, including English and Americans, had assembled to see the sight. Such a crowd and press and chattering as there was—such a mixture of priests and sisters, with a stray Cardinal occasionally, and the young Neapolitan princesses to add to the interest of the scene! I have not possibly time to describe it all; but it was a very real thing, though very odd to English eyes. The Pilgrims were really wretched, and the sisters really washed their feet, and waited upon them. They come as a matter of religious duty— the pilgrims, I mean—and the sisters wait upon them as an act of penance. It seems peculiar to have a great crowd of strangers looking on, but one must not judge Italians by our English standard.

Easter Tuesday.—Since I wrote this I have seen St. Peter's illuminated—most glorious it was!

A palace of light, with dim stone columns before it, rising up into the dark sky; the stars quietly shining above, and the fountains looking like falling—I don't know what to call them—only in that light they were fountains etherealized. We saw it from the Piazza and the Pincian Hill. From the hill, Rome lay all dark below us, save here and there a few scattered lights, and the traces of a lighted street, the lamps of which were hidden. In the centre was St. Peter's glittering and sparkling; the focus to which all things were converging. Since the illumination, (the next morning,) I have seen the Pope and Cardinals coming from a consistory in the Vatican, and have been through the interminable halls and long corridors, filled with sculpture and ornamented with marble and fountains; and I have seen the Apollo Belvedere, and I have also had the most enchanting drive, with views of the Sabine mountains, the pine trees, and cypresses of Rome —more soft and lovely than words can tell—and now my letter *must* go.   Yours, &c., &c.

P.S.—You will see that I have said nothing about Easter Sunday, which is the great day for the ceremonies at St. Peter's; but the fact is that we found it impossible to make them fit in with our own services. I confess I should like to have heard the blast of the silver trumpets at a particular part of the Mass. People say it is a sound so thrilling, but so sweet, that one could neither imagine nor forget it.

I have taken this letter as giving the *feeling* of the rush and excitement which, I suppose, are almost inseparable from the Holy Week at Rome, and I must make it my text-book for a few remarks.

And first, with regard to the Miserere. My idea, and therefore probably that of many others, was that the Miserere was a service performed on a certain day, in a certain place, but this is not the case. The Miserere, being the Fifty-first Psalm, is chanted on the Thursday and Friday, as well as on the Wednesday, in Holy Week, and it may be heard at St. Peter's as well as at the Sistine Chapel.

The choice of the day and the place is a topic for musical discussion in the Roman world. There are several Misereres, by several composers, and you select your favourite, and go where you think you will hear the best performance. After our struggle in the Sistine Chapel we found ourselves the next afternoon at St. Peter's, comfortably seated in the little gallery in the Capella del Coro, listening to another Miserere, and able to enter into it without any of the disturbing associations of the preceding day. Probably the best performance was at the

Sistine, and certainly at St. Peter's the music was more modern, and though excessively sweet, not so devotional, but this was merely accidental; and unquestionably, if I were to be in Rome again, I would willingly yield any superiority which may rest with the Sistine music, for the sake of the quietness and freedom from annoyance which are experienced at St. Peter's. In both places I was entirely disappointed in the effect of the service. I had heard of the awful impression produced by the extinction of the lights, one by one, as the Miserere is chanted; but, although candles are put out, light remains. The ugly square windows of the Sistine chapel admit quite enough to destroy any feeling of solemnity; and at St. Peter's I should only have remarked a little dimness. The Capella del Coro is in itself so light, that a few candles more or less make very little difference; and the attempt to bring before the mind the darkness which covered the earth at our Blessed Lord's death, utterly fails. So again at the conclusion of the service a noise is made which is intended to represent the confusion of nature when "the earth trembled and the rocks were rent;" but to my ears it was nothing but a theatrical clattering for about a minute, followed by the rush to the door of priests and people, seemingly thankful that it was all over. I say this in, I hope, no criticising or irreverent spirit. If the subject to which the service referred had been peculiarly Romish, I could have looked on with comparative indifference; but being, as it was, that which Christians of every shade of opinion agree in recognising with the deepest awe, anything which led one to the edge of the fatal step "from the sublime to the ridiculous" was necessarily most painful.

The different effect produced by the Pauline Chapel was owing to the fact that there was no attempt to represent anything. The symbol on the altar was all the more impressive because it was only a symbol—that it suggested no comparison between representation and reality.

There were other ceremonies, and very important ones, on the Thursday in Holy Week, which I did not attempt, and indeed felt no wish to see, being quite sure that they would excite the same jarred sensation as the scenic darkness and the mock thunder in the Sistine Chapel. At the conclusion of the benediction given from the balcony, the Pope descends to the right-hand transept of St. Peter's, and there washes the feet of thirteen priests, who are supposed to represent the twelve Apostles, with a thirteenth, who once appeared miraculously to Gregory the Great when he was performing a similar ceremony. After this the thirteen priests dine in the gallery over the portico, and the Pope waits upon them.

To hear these things discussed in a light way,

and questions asked as to whether you have tickets for the *Lavanda* or the *Tavola,* or for both, and then to consider what the real meaning of these ceremonies is, and Whom the Pope professes to represent, is too painful to admit even of any sense of the ludicrous. Yet that is the tone which persons who have been present usually adopt when speaking of the religious sights of the Thursday in Holy Week.

The Lavanda at the Trinità dei Pellegrini is a totally different thing. If I had been able to plan my day beforehand, I should not indeed have chosen the evening of Good Friday for the excitement of such a scene, but when I returned home I had no sense of mockery or unreality. Whatever were the unavoidable accompaniments of crowd and confusion, the action itself was unmistakeably self-denying and charitable. The pilgrims, who have certificates from their priests, come from a distance, to perform what they consider acts of devotion. They are received at the Hospital; and for three days,—the Wednesday, Thursday, and Friday in Holy Week,—the noble ladies of Rome devote themselves, at special times, to the duty of attending upon the women; while cardinals, priests, and nobles wait upon the men. And the duty—so far as I could form any opinion— was very carefully and tenderly performed. The ladies, distinguished by their dress, paid no regard to the crowd. There were tables set out in the rooms into which we at first entered; the space which they occupied being separated by a cord from the rest of the apartment. Within this space passed young girls, with bright and pleasant faces, carrying trays of lettuce and fish; without, were elderly ladies—princesses and countesses—striving to act the part of police, and keep back the mob of bonnets and crinolines which was striving to press forward to the scene of the Lavanda. Priests, dressed, I am compelled to own, very like cooks, now and then appeared, but they took no part in the regulations. My small experience has led me to the conclusion that a crowd of wilful and pushing women is more unmanageable than a similar crowd of men; and I greatly admired the lady who kept guard between two of the rooms, admitting only a few of us at a time, and then quietly closing the door, and placing herself with her back to it, smiling at us in the most good-natured way, though with an air of determination which plainly showed that she did not intend to be trifled with. When at length we were permitted to pass, we were directed to descend into a lower apartment, which might have been a large scullery or wash-house. The pilgrims were seated on raised benches, and the ladies—chiefly young girls—knelt before them.

In the centre stood a bishop, reading some prayers, to which a response was every now and then given. The degradation, the mixture of poverty, and, in some cases, almost imbecility and idiotcy of the beggars, their unutterable dirt, the tainted atmosphere of the room, and the damp heat, must have rendered the duty of the delicate, refined-looking girls an undertaking almost beyond endurance. One, who was waiting upon a singularly wretched looking creature, looked as if she was upon the point of fainting; but she finished her task, the woman put on her stockings—I am sorry to say the same which had been taken off, and which alone must have rendered the ablution nearly useless, especially as no soap seemed allowed—and then she left the room, leaning on the arm of the young girl, who evinced no feeling of repulsion, but took the poor creature under her care, and led her through the crowd with a simple devotion to the self-imposed duty which was most touching.

Compared with this the Papal washing at St. Peter's must be a distressing mockery. We did not stay for the supper which is given after the Lavanda. A few minutes in such an atmosphere was more than sufficient: and what must it have been to the persons actually engaged in the work!

I had a short discussion with a gentleman whom

I very much respected, as to the spirit with which an action of this kind was likely to be performed. He thought that a love of display must mingle with it; and looked upon it in the light of the precept, " Do not your alms before men to be seen of them." It did not strike me in the same way. The manner of the persons engaged was, for the most part, singularly simple,—and there were too many to allow of a feeling of superiority to others. Then the crowd was so great and so mixed,—the greater number were foreigners, who could not have known one "sister" from another. Abstractedly, I should agree that to perform a penitential act in the sight of curious spectators, without ostentation, was impossible; but what I saw that evening has shaken my faith in abstract judgments. And one thing I am sure we ought always to take into consideration when judging the religion of continental nations,—they are brought up in publicity as regards devotion. From their early childhood they are accustomed to go into a church, and kneel down to their prayers without the least thought of singularity or observation. It is to them as much a matter of course as it is for us to attend a public service on Sundays; and the same spirit follows them, I suspect, through life. The English shrinking from being talked about, being unlike one's neighbours, is not an element in their nature; and as they have less shyness, so, as a natural consequence, they have less display.

To me, it would certainly seem that the Lavanda at the Trinità dei Pellegrini is not intended in the least for show, but for a public recognition of the combined duties of personal humility and sympathy with the needs of the poor and suffering,—a recognition which could not be made if the act was done in secret. That there are many more such charitable deeds performed privately, by the very same persons who, on this one occasion, wait upon the pilgrims, is, I believe, generally acknowledged. To endeavour to enter into the spirit of other persons' actions is, however, very different from wishing to imitate them. The last thing I should desire would be to see a ceremony like the Lavanda introduced into England. The mere fact that it was a novelty would, when combined with our national self-consciousness, destroy its simplicity; and a religious act which is not simple must be as unimpressive to the spectators as it is injurious to the participators.

As a strange conclusion to the sights of a Good Friday in Rome, we stopped, as we were returning from the Lavanda, to look at the illuminated pork shops in the neighbourhood of the Pantheon and the Piazza Navona. They are intended as a mark of insult to the Jews. The lights are placed so as to display ceilings of hams and cheeses, and arabesques of lard mosaicised; whilst, at the farther extremity, sausages and other similar eatables surround brilliant little shrines containing images of the Virgin. This, like the other sights of the Holy Week, is not confined exclusively to Good Friday. It may be seen also on the Thursday; and a person anxious to understand Rome and Roman customs, yet desirous of having a very quiet Good Friday, might by consideration beforehand, and proper arrangement of time, avoid the disturbance and incongruity of sight-seeing on such a day.

CHAPTER XII.

EASTER Tuesday was marked by my first visit to the Vatican, and that suggests the most difficult of the many subjects connected with Rome,—art, exhibited both in sculpture and painting. The common inquiry made when a traveller returns from Rome is, What did you think of the pictures? Did you admire the Apollo? Were you satisfied with the Dying Gladiator, &c. &c.? And every one seems to expect in reply some original and striking criticism. There may be some competent to give such criticism, but the chief wish of ignorant and unartistic persons must—so it appears to me—be, to look, and enjoy, and form their own opinions, and be permitted to keep them to themselves. The very fact of agreement with a universal judgment destroys the pleasure one feels in the formation of such a judgment. To know beforehand that you must admire the Apollo, makes you shrink from saying anything about it. You doubt your own sincerity if you are following the multitude; and if you do not follow it—if from any peculiarity of taste or character you stand aloof, and venture to condemn what others appreciate—you are instantly called upon to analyse and explain, perhaps to bring forth hidden and sacred feelings and associations, scarcely recognised by yourself, and utterly inexplicable to the majority of your hearers.

Another consciousness which I suspect is more common than people are apt to acknowledge, is that of not knowing what one does think, not only about art, but about a vast number of other subjects. No doubt it would be a most excellent practice for us all, if we were to accustom ourselves so to examine our own impressions as to understand and explain the grounds of our judgment. It may be that to comprehend ourselves, would, in art as well as in morals, be the first step towards comprehending others; it may be that we cannot be said to know any subject until we have thus examined and defined the effect it has produced upon us; but it is quite certain that the effort which such an examination and definition requires is by no means slight, and that the majority of persons are far too indolent to make it. That the effort will be greater or less, according to the taste and character of the individual, will at once be acknowledged. A real artist, a heaven-born artist, will find no difficulty in deciding why such or such a picture is pleasing to him, or the reverse; but very few persons are heaven-born artists. Of the hundreds who crowd the galleries of the Vatican every winter, perhaps not above two or three can lay claim to the title. The remainder have no opinions at all, or none which are worthy to be so called. That this is the fact we may all, unless numbered amongst the exceptions, have a convincing proof by inquiring what decided recollections and what confirmed judgments we retained six months after our visit to a studio or a gallery of paintings. For myself, in looking back upon my Roman and Florentine experience of art, it is an actual grief to me to find how very vague and indefinite are the impressions which have been made upon me. At the moment I liked or disliked, I admired or criticised; but I was too constantly engaged to have leisure for reflection. I was conscious of the impression, but I had neither the time nor the energy to convert it into an opinion, and in consequence it is gone.

The Apollo Belvedere is an exception to this remark. I do know what I thought about that, because I took the trouble to inquire at the time. It surpassed my expectations, because it made me *feel*. Generally speaking, heathen statues of gods and goddesses leave me as cold as the marble in which they are sculptured. But the Apollo is a perfect expression of human divinity, if one may be allowed the phrase. It has eternal youth, undying life, untiring, unwasting energy. It has an impulse which can never slacken, an aim which can never be satisfied, which must be always reaching forward, always claiming new power, new dominion. The attitude and the countenance describe the same characteristics. Shut out the face, and look only at the figure—yet you feel what the face must be. It has never known, it never can know, sorrow; but so also it can never know compassion,—it can never be softened by sympathy; and in gazing at it the mind instinctively recurs to One who with man's nature took also his infirmities, and the difference between the heathen and the Christian God comes home to the heart with a thrill of unutterable thankfulness.

The Apollo has one great advantage in standing alone in a cabinet expressly appropriated to it, and with a background of colour which especially suits it. Indeed, the great charm of the Vatican is, that the statues are admirably placed, and that the whole range of the halls and galleries is calculated to exhibit them in the most perfect way. They are not rooms built for the reception of the statues, but magnificent apartments, of which the statues are the ornament. The two are, in idea, inseparable. As you traverse the marble floors, and pass through open courts and porticoes, listening to the soothing gush of the ever-springing fountain, you feel that in Italy art is one with the people,—it is indigenous;

and a palace without sculpture, would be as unnatural and impossible as a palace without furniture. I was especially sensible of this when I saw the Vatican by torchlight. A party was made for the purpose, and we went, about eight o'clock in the evening, passing through the scene of our conflict with the Swiss guards, who looked quite tame, as, wrapped in their great coats, they hovered round braziers of charcoal, trying to keep themselves from the cold blasts, which even in Rome may be felt in the month of April. Our guide took with him a huge torch hidden by a shade, so that the light was cast effectively; and as we followed through the long galleries, the exquisite effects were even more striking, to me, than the light thrown upon the statues. There was a softness and richness of colouring and material which it would be quite impossible to find in our papered rooms. Polished dark marble columns, sarcophagi, vases, and mosaic floors gleamed as the light fell upon them, and then were multiplied by imagination as they passed into darkness; and amidst them the graceful groups of statuary—the stern marble faces of bygone deities, and buried emperors, and statesmen looked forth upon us, as if reproaching us for the irreverence which had led us to intrude into the halls which were theirs by right and inheritance, far more than by mere possession.

The statues in the Museum of the Capitol have by no means an equal advantage in point of situation with those in the Vatican. The galleries and rooms are nothing more than might be found in other places; and it was only when I turned from the Dying Gladiator to look from the window at the dark red walls of the ruined Coliseum, that I felt that the statue belonged to Rome, and could never find its fitting resting-place except where those walls could be kept in view. That same room contains the gems of the collection;—the exquisite little statue of a girl playing with a dove, and terrified at the approach of a snake, which was the one thing I could have carried away with a clear conscience as regarded fitness, and placed in my own home; the Antinous, which, though repeated again and again in other Roman collections, struck me as never being so perfect as in this representation; and the Faun, which to the readers and admirers of Hawthorne's "Transformation" must have received a new and lasting interest. It is so exactly what it is there described, that it would be useless to make any comment upon it. The collection of sculptures in the Capitol gave me a longing, which was very frequently awakened in Rome, to be able to study with all the aids which are to be found there. The busts of the long line of Emperors seem to bring them before you as if yet living; and it is tantalizing to pass from one to the other, conscious what a world of thought might be awakened by them, and yet to be unable to give more than a momentary glance, and that perhaps destructive of all one's preconceived ideas. The ugly countenance of Titus, and the thoughtful, eager, very remarkable, though not handsome face of Julian, imprinted themselves especially on my memory. Certainly Rome is the city of sculpture, as Florence is of painting. The Borghese, Ludovisi, and Albani Villas are crowded with statues, vases, and bas-reliefs; but the eye at last grows weary of them —an *embarras de richesses* ceases to afford pleasure; and in these private collections the good and the bad are so intermixed, that you are tired of looking at indifferent specimens before you have reached that which is really good. Upon the whole, the sculptures at the Villas possessed but little attraction for me, though there are some most beautiful things to be found amongst them.

Modern sculpture is another very large subject of Roman interest. Every one talks about it, and every one knows some one who *dabbles* in it. Sculpture and the excavations seemed to me to be, in Rome, what law cases are to a barrister, and classes and degrees to an Oxonian; they formed the small talk of society, and though, as usual, they became after a time rather vapid, yet it is a sign of the charm which Rome possesses, above all other places, that even the little nothings which it suggests have in them the germs of really valuable information. The studios are open to every one, and are as necessary a part of sight-seeing as the Vatican or the Capitol; and people are less afraid of giving an opinion upon them than upon ancient art. It would be heretical to criticise the Apollo, but one may fairly be allowed to pass judgment upon Gibson's coloured statue of Venus, or Pandora. I believe I am in the minority in saying that I admire them,—the Pandora especially. I should not like to see colouring commonly introduced into sculpture; it seems to require a delicacy of taste which must be very rare, and which, if wanting, would render the attempt a fatal failure. A coloured statue which is not beautiful must be a monstrosity. It would be a representation, not a suggestion; and so, like the theatrical Romish ceremonies, would excite a sense of the ridiculous. But the charm in Gibson's statues is exactly this, that they are suggestive. Pandora is not a woman with a flesh-coloured complexion and black eyes, but an exquisite creation of a being so human and life-like as to touch one's sympathies, yet so ethereal in the tint which is shed over her, that she is felt to be as yet unsullied by the evil to which ordinary mortality is heir. Only in the sweet sorrow of her most lovely face can be read the foreboding of the consequences of her own rashness. I saw two other very perfect statues in the studio of Mr. Story, an American gentleman,—Cleopatra, and the Libyan Sybil. In both there was a careful observance of the Egyptian type of countenance and style of dress,—and I was surprised to see how extremely beautiful they could be. Cleopatra is generally represented as a Greek, and it is difficult to imagine her anything else; but the Egyptian features, and the low ornamental fillet—to an English taste, generally so destructive of beauty—certainly did not in this case in the least detract from her charms. The Sybil was wonderful,—so earnest, thoughtful, sorrowful,—so impressed with the weight of her own powers, and so very beautiful—yet not in the least according to any regularly acknowledged type of beauty; exaggerate the features or the expression in the slightest degree, and she might be repulsive, even coarse.

There is one studio in Rome which every one visits, as much for the sake of the artist as his works —Overbeck's. Whatever may be the variety of opinions as to the drawings, there can be but one as to the man himself. It might almost be said indeed, that if any person ever deserved to succeed in an attempt from the spirit in which he entered upon it, it would be one who is so especially and supereminently Christian in his tone of mind. We found him at work, with Scripture subjects surrounding him, and he himself—dressed in a loose robe and a velvet cap—ready to receive us with the simplicity, earnestness, and spirituality which one might have imagined as belonging to the days of the Apostles. He is now an old man, with a thin, worn face, remarkable for its repose and sweetness. His manners are devoid of the slightest taint of self-consciousness. As he went from picture to picture, explaining the typical meaning of the subjects he had chosen, he seemed to lose all thought of his work as work, and to regard it solely as an expression of religious feeling. And as sketches, his designs are beautiful; he seems to delight in gathering types and illustrations around one central idea, as in his drawings for the seven sacraments, where he collects in medallions around the centre all the subjects from the Old Testament which may be supposed to have reference to them. Finished pictures from these sketches were, he said, originally a commission from Vienna, but the state of the country had interfered with the completion of the proposal. For myself, I would far rather have the sketches. Overbeck fails when he attempts to finish. His colouring is weak, and his outline hard. He spoke very affectionately of his son-in-law Hoffman, the sculptor, who resides in the same house; and was most anxious that we should see his studio. It was so delightful, he said, to have a person living with him who shared his tastes and devoted himself only to sacred subjects,—and when I saw the studio I quite understood the old man's satisfaction. Instead of being surrounded by gods and goddesses of very indifferent character, to find oneself in the midst of objects which one could really dwell upon with reverence, was a great, though, I doubt not, a very un-artistic gratification. The Apollo may be immeasurably superior to Hoffman's figure of St. John, reclining on our Lord's breast, and learning from Him the mystery of the Trinity; yet an effort of mind was required before one could *feel* the beauty of the one, whilst the other touched the heart instantaneously. The figure of St. John was often repeated. I can imagine his character singularly suiting the temperament of Overbeck, and probably therefore of the son-in-law who so sympathises with him. An unfinished Hagar and Ishmael, and a very beautiful St. Joseph, also struck me much; and there was a Piétâ, which Overbeck told us was one of Hoffman's best works. Sadness there is in all these subjects, and sadness is for the most part absent from the creations of heathenism; but this only proves that its ideal, if not Divine, was certainly not human. It ignored, because it dared not face, sorrow; and which of us in moments of faithlessness is not even now tempted to do the same?

Painting in Rome is, upon the whole, disappointing. Some magnificent pictures no doubt there are, and the Vatican collection is, I imagine, unrivalled; but then it is extremely small. There are but fifty pictures in the whole, and though this adds in one respect to the pleasure of seeing them, since one is not so overpowered as in large galleries, yet it does not satisfy the idea of lavishness, which is naturally associated with Italian art. And they have no advantage from locality. The long stone corridors and staircases, which are traversed and ascended before reaching the gallery, have nothing in the slightest degree interesting or beautiful in them; and when at length you enter the suite of rather low rooms, very high up, the idea which presents itself is rather that of good-sized upper chambers in a private house than of a gallery for the *chef-d'œuvres* of art.

The one great satisfaction in visiting the Vatican gallery is, however, the sense of repose. There is no rushing from one treasure to another with the fear of overlooking what ought to be seen, and receiving such a variety of impressions, that it is impossible to retain distinctly any one in particular. There are two charming Murillos in the first room—the Return of the Prodigal Son, and the Marriage of St. Catherine—which strike the eye directly, because they are so un-Italian. This is especially the case with the St. Catherine. The dark hair and brilliant eyes, and the power and energy mingled with womanly grace and delicacy, form a beauty which may be less ethereal than one is accustomed to associate with sacred subjects, but I think it excites and interests one more. And the same may be said of Murillo's Madonnas, which have a similar character. Comparing them with Raphael's they seem earthly, but it is an earthliness which has the capability of greater elevation than the gentle but passive loveliness, the principal charm of which lies in the expression of youthful maternal love. The second room has but three pictures; I think I should be better pleased if there were but two. Raphael's Madonna del Foligno is not, as a whole, satisfactory. It is one of those singular religious and historical medleys in which saints, and ordinary human beings with very material human interests, are brought together so as to touch no possible chord of sympathy; and the unity of the picture is destroyed by a very beautiful, but very intrusive little angel, who holds a tablet in his hand, with no object but that of recording a date and the name of the artist and his patron.

Raphael's Transfiguration, and Domenichino's Communion of St. Jerome, are well worthy to stand alone. Prints of the Transfiguration give not the least idea of the perfection of the picture. The colouring alone is so admirable, that it leaves nothing to be desired. At a first glance I had not the least wish to criticise; and though when I examined it more closely, I felt dissatisfied with the floating figures of Moses and Elijah, it seemed almost wrong to dwell upon defects when the centre delineation of our Lord was so wonderful, and the story of the demoniac boy in the foreground described with such life-like vividness.

The Communion of St. Jerome has not the peculiar touch which Raphael always gives—the delicacy which belongs to him alone; and most expressive as the countenances are, there is no single face which seizes upon the imagination with that sense of beauty before unrealized, which is awakened only by him; but it tells its tale instantly and most forcibly. The few figures are living and breathing men and women; their thoughts and feelings are portrayed so plainly, that by studying the picture you could almost put them into words. It has no exaggeration, no straining after effect, and there are no anachronisms to disturb its truthfulness. As St. Jerome really looked and spoke in his last moments, so you feel that you see him looking and speaking now; the representation might be a photograph of the real scene.

And very lovely pictures there are in the rooms beyond — works of Perugino, Moretto, Titian, Pinturiccho, &c., and a magnificent Guido,—the Crucifixion of St. Peter. Yet there is an attraction in the Raphael and the Domenichino which is continually drawing one back to look at them once more. These solitary pictures of Raphael gave me a real delight in him; but the far-famed Stanze and Loggie disappointed me. First of all they are frescoes, and frescoes, even in Italy, are always fading; but even if they were not, the inspection, at least of the Loggie, must be, to a person not blessed with remarkable physical powers, a very painful enjoyment. The Loggie themselves are indeed open arcades, elaborately ornamented with arabesques and stucco ornaments, and are easily seen, and very much to be admired; but the beautiful frescoes are in the roofs of the arcades; and what it is to stand on a hot day, with upraised head and strained eyes, to gaze at pictures, the subjects of which can with difficulty be descried, I need not say. The Stanze are large empty rooms, the walls of which were painted by Raphael, and his peculiar beauty in design and his exquisite finish are very evident; but with the exception of the well-known "Expulsion of Heliodorus from the Temple," no one picture left any impression upon me such as would make me greatly desire to see it again; and this, I think, is the real test of the effect produced.

The remaining pictures in Rome are scattered in palaces and churches. The Borghese, Doria, Colonna, Corsini, and Sciarra Galleries, are the best; and whilst they contain a good deal which is uninteresting, there are also to be found in them pictures which linger in the memory like the thought of the few friends who have become an actual part of one's life. They have assisted to form the taste—they have been real masters and teachers, placing before the mind a standard, which without them would have been unimaginable. Some of Raphael's portraits are of this kind; and there are two of that very rare master Leonardo da Vinci;—one called Modesty and Vanity, in the Sciarra Gallery, and another in the Doria,—Joanna the Second of Naples. If the likeness is good—and there can be no reason, I suppose, to doubt it—Joanna would seem to have been Leonardo's model of female beauty, for the face is repeated by him continually, until at last indeed one is weary of it. The great charm in the "Modesty" in the former picture is, that the countenance has all Leonardo's finish, without any of his mannerism. "Vanity" is Joanna degenerated. Guido's Aurora, a fresco in the Rospigliosi Palace, must also be specially mentioned. It is supposed to be well known because it is so often copied and photographed; but there could scarcely be a greater mistake than to imagine that any copy, much less any photograph, could give an idea of the beauty of the original. The grace of the figures may be retained, but the brilliancy of the colouring, as seen through a glass, which reflects the frescoes on the ceiling, could never, I should think, be conveyed either by oil or water colours.

CHAPTER XIII.

The centre of Rome, between the foreigners' section and the ruins, is by far the most imposing portion of the modern city. It was indeed the only part which at all came up to my preconceived ideas of Roman grandeur and solemnity; for here the palaces are concentrated, and in them are to be found the massive architecture and ornamented façades which are required to produce an effect of stability and wealth. Many of the palaces are indeed falling to decay in the interior, and look dreary in their deserted grandeur; but the Borghese, the Doria, and the Colonna are still splendid, with long suites of rooms and gilded galleries, rich in tables and vases of marble. I think it was in the Palazzo Colonna that I saw lying on the ground, in a most magnificent Salle, a cannon ball. It had been permitted to remain there, on the exact spot on which it had fallen, since the French siege in 1849,—a record which made one feel that one was living in historical times. The Palazzo Spada, most uninteresting in itself, possesses a treasure, which to me was almost unequalled in interest,— the statue of Pompey, associated for ever with the murder of Cæsar. It is true that critics have, as usual, discussed its authenticity, until one is compelled to make an effort and determine to believe before one can quite be enthusiastic about it; but as inquiry has only served to establish its claim, and as it is one of those cases in which credulity—if it be credulity—is an error which brings much pleasure and no pain, I for one chose to look at it as the very identical statue, and to give myself up to the enjoyment of that peculiar feeling of living at some marked period, centuries before one's real earthly existence began, which is only awakened when actual touch and sight create a link between that age and the present moment. What the life in the interior of these palaces is, the outer world is not allowed to judge. It would seem that the Roman nobles take very little part in public matters. How, indeed, should they, when they can have little or no voice in them? Prince Doria, I was told, sympathises with the Liberal movement. He has erected in the grounds of the Villa Pamphili Doria—which it must be remembered is a *maison de campagne*, distinct from the Palace—a monument to the memory of the French soldiers who, in 1849, fell in the conflicts that took place in the neighbourhood; but whether sympathy with the French is sympathy with liberalism or despotism, who, in these days, can venture to decide? Having married an English wife, he may, however, naturally be supposed to have English sympathies. Certainly the gardens of his villa are entirely English in their character, and are kept, not according to the French idea of a *jardin Anglais*, which generally means dark overgrown trees and untidy walks, but with a neatness which is a perfect rest to the eye. The same taste is visible in the Borghese Villa, the general resort for the fashionable world on a Sunday afternoon, and very delightful at all times. There are drives both in the Borghese and the Pamphili Doria grounds which might belong to an English park; they have all the freshness, luxuriance, and enchanting verdure of England, with the additional charm of the clear sky and soft air of Italy. But there is melancholy connected with them—with the Pamphili Doria especially—the fatal malaria is so prevalent, though the villa is only about half a mile from the Porta S. Pancrazio, that it can only be inhabited for a few months in the year, and this is the case with many of the villas about Rome; and after visiting them, one is apt to ask oneself why so much thought and money should be expended upon them.

To our English ideas the pleasure of going to a country house, about a mile out of the city, and spending the day without any particular object except that of being cool, must be very doubtful.

Home associations would seem to be impossible; and so, in all these villas, there is an entire absence of anything which would suggest the idea of permanent interest. You see few tables, no books; the ceilings and walls are beautifully painted, and there are lovely specimens of marble,—but the cold white statues are the only inhabitants. Yet it is ungrateful to complain. The Pamphili Doria is a fairyland for the visitors of Rome, and open to them at all times; and the view from one of the entrance gates looking over St. Peter's to Soracte, is alone sufficient to make one linger there with delight. In views like this is to be found the great charm of all the Roman villas. Everywhere indeed are the same materials for the landscape; but seen from different points, and under different effects of sky and atmosphere, they form an ever-varying and ever-beautiful series of satisfying pictures.

From the top of the house at the Pamphili Doria the eye passes to the Campagna and the hills, over a foreground of enriched ornamental garden, —terraces, marble balustrades, vases, and flowers, backed by the luxuriant foliage of the trees in the extensive grounds, where all shades of green are mingled with the rich pink lilac of the Judas tree, nowhere to be seen in greater beauty. In a grove apart, the tall sombre pines, the "islands in the sky," stand out in proud contrast with the blue heavens; and as they gently sway to and fro, and the breeze wakens the soft moan which seems the whisper of sorrow, one feels how singularly they accord with the spirit of the city to which they belong. Like so many other things in Rome, they have a voice and meaning there, which—transplant them—and they must lose for ever. A Roman pine apart from Rome is the exile of exiles.

Another view which I recall with delight was from the roof of the Ludovisi Villa, where, however, the statues are generally considered the great attraction. The sky on that particular day was cloudy, almost stormy, and the hills from Soracte to the Alban Mount were all dark and purple, except where a pale, sunny green light gleamed down the slope above Frascati, and touched the white villas and houses, and then wound in amongst the valleys, carrying the eye on, from one range of hills to another, till the peaks of the Sabine mountains in the far distance, on which the sun was resting, blended with the clouds, and the outline of earth was lost in the hazy sky which, though it is nowise heaven, yet is to us its border-land. The effect which all such views produce is that of melancholy, real, yet sweet and very soothing. For there is no sternness in the scenery about Rome, least of all in the mountains. They gather round the Campagna with the loving tenderness of a mother, rather than the powerful protection of a father. The strength of their outline is softened by the delicacy of their colouring; and as they recede one behind another, the mind travels amongst them with a feeling of seeking and finding not only beauty, but rest.

The Campagna spreads before the eye a waste of shadows and varying tints, floating over it like a veil with which it is striving to hide the ruin that lies beneath. The city, solemn, decayed, yet living and restless, burdens the heart with its centuries of degradation; but away amongst the hills there is no ruin, no degradation. What the Alban Mount, the Sabine mountains, and the lovely Soracte are now, they were in the days of Rome's first greatness, and they will be when—if ever—her name has ceased to be a centre of interest for the civilized world; and so when thought is weary, and association is oppressive, the sight of them gives that sense of stability and repose which can only be found in scenes from which man is absent, and where God is ever-present.

Notwithstanding the unhealthiness of many of the Roman villas, there are, however, some unhaunted by the spectre of malaria; and which, without having any pretensions to magnificence, would afford ample scope for enjoyment. The Villa Mellini, on Monte Mario, which forms so prominent an object from the Pincian Hill, is one of these. Its reputation as regards health, is not indeed untainted; but, as far as I could learn, it would be more possible to live there than in other villas even nearer to the city. The house shares the natural ugliness of Italian domestic architecture, but it would be a most agreeable summer home. When once the labour of ascending the steep winding road was over, it would seem possible to enjoy months in taking in and thoroughly understanding all that is to be seen from the terrace. The city lies immediately below;—not the old ruined Rome, the position of which is, however, clearly marked by the Coliseum, which from every point around Rome is seen,—the very giant of decay, towering above the surrounding buildings,—but the modern foreigners' Rome, strangely mingled with records of far distant ages, such as the Ponte Molle, which crosses the winding, yellow Tiber at some little distance from the city, and is famous as the spot where Catiline's conspirators were taken. When seen from the hill of Monte Mario, all idea of the individual elevation of the seven hills of Rome is lost. The whole city appears built upon a raised table-land, stretching out into the Campagna. The long white façade of the Quirinal stands out plainly, but the streets and houses which crowd around it interfere with the idea of height. The Pincian, though so near, looks artificial, from the walls and arches which are built up round it. But there is nothing tamer or disappointing in this view of the great city. Ages in Rome mingle and embrace so remarkably, that the bareness of the present is always softened and poetised by the past. The regular masonry of the modern Pincian, for instance, blends with the deep-tinted, ivy-covered old walls which surround the city, and which are in themselves a history. And if at one moment the associations of the foreign fashionable life force themselves upon you disagreeably, you have but to carry your glance across the city and the Campagna to the steep outline which forms the termination of the Sabine range, and in the white spot just seen at the foot of the hills, and at the opening of the level country extending in the direction of Terracina, you will recognise a place which acknowledged a king long before Rome was founded, and where still are to be seen walls built with enormous polygonal masses of stone,—the characteristic of the architecture of the Pelasgi. With Palestrina in sight, even though it may only be seen as a speck, one can scarcely complain of a view as devoid of interest.

And there is one beauty, the newest, freshest, youngest of all, which I recognised on the day when I visited the Villa Mellini, and which can never be unsuitable, never disturb the mind with the sense of incongruity,—the beauty of early spring. So strange it is to see how God, in nature, can harmonize all things most discordant!—how, as in the mystery of Eternity, age and youth may meet and blend, and Time be in thought annihilated. The fresh tendrils that now cling to the old walls of Rome are one with them as truly as were those early tender branches which first found a resting-place in their crevices. Gifted with an ever-renewed youth, they add to rather than detract from the veneration inspired by age; and apart from them antiquity too often becomes repulsive. And so it was that the early budding trees, with their vivid green leaves sparkling like drops of light, which clothed the sides of Monte Mario, and beyond which rose the domes and towers of the city, its ruined walls and decayed palaces, and the mountains tipped with snow, were felt to be but a natural and suitable framework for the landscape. Adjuncts and ornaments they were, which, if planned by man, might have jarred against the spirit of the view; but which coming from the Hand of God were acknowledged to be only the expression of the truth underlying all ruin and all death,—even resurrection and immortality.

And one more Villa I must name, not because of its splendour, its vastness, or even its antiquity, but because, when I think of it, it summons up the one cherished English thought of home,—home in Italy, with all its accessories of painting, sculpture, and relics of the past. It is a home which will soon be, even if it is not now, invaded, perhaps destroyed, for it is threatened with a railway in its near vicinity; but such as it was when I was introduced to it I would fain describe it. It was not an English home;—a deserted palace, with empty vaulted corridors bearing the marks of faded frescoes on the walls, uninhabited chambers, and endlessly ascending stone staircases, could never in England be an ideal of home. But when, leaving all these behind, and passing through a quaint ante-room—half passage, half servants' sitting-room, and wholly Italian—you entered the large Salle, with its crimson paper and vaulted papered ceiling, its sofas, ottomans, books, statuettes, and copies of first-rate pictures—Guido's sketches of angels, Titian's Bella Donna—with others personal and domestic, you were at once transplanted into the home atmosphere in which all cherished feelings could expand without check. Such a room in an Italian palace must be as rare as it is fascinating. But the garden and the view from the windows an Italian would assuredly claim as his own. Where in England, or America—for the friend who made the villa her residence was an American—could be seen the avenue of tall cypresses, swaying to and fro, soothingly yet funereally; the long walks bordered by orange trees, and terminated by high gates of iron open work, the formal parterres surrounded by box hedges, the trickling fountains, and broken statues? Where, in England or America, could it be possible to sit at the window of one's own drawing-room, and gaze at leisure upon a scene fraught with such associations; its prominent objects the dome of S. Maria Maggiore, the Church of St. John Lateran, the Coliseum, the remains of the Temple of Minerva Medica, the ruins of an aqueduct, and the mound clothed with cedars, where may still be seen traces of the ancient wall of Servius Tullius; whilst beyond rise the snow-covered hills of the Sabines, and the mount upon which once stood the city of Alba Longa?

Description can give no idea of the feeling which such a home must create. Decayed, deserted though it is, yet the mournful beauty sinks into the heart, and leaves an ineffaceable impression. The loveliness which springs from ruin, like the peace to be found in sorrow, must be felt to be understood.

CHAPTER XIV.

46, *Via Sistina, April,* 1861.

My dear ——,

E—— asks me in one note to tell her about public matters: the fact is, we know no more about them here than you do in England. The reports are just as variable, and just as little to be depended upon. The Pope has been ill,—that you will have seen in the papers. We happened to be at the Vatican in the Sala Regia, which is a vestibule to the Sistine Chapel, at the very moment when he was passing through it hurriedly, just before he fainted. Several Cardinals were with him, Antonelli amongst them. I caught a glimpse of his dark, handsome face, which has much more power than the generality of Cardinalistic countenances. Whether it may be the dress which is so unimposing, or whether, as a class, they really are undignified, I certainly never saw any men holding high office, either in Church or State, to whom, as regards outward appearance, one should be less willing to yield reverence. They may have been of a different stamp in former days. To judge by some of Raphael's portraits, they were, but even then the expression tells of sharp worldly wisdom far more than piety. The Pope himself I did not see plainly on that particular occasion, but I had had a full view of him before, on the day when he went to St. Peter's, and performed his devotions publicly—praying at different altars, and kissing the toe of the black statue, which once was Jupiter, and now is St. Peter. He is just like his pictures, not at all dignified, but apparently simply earnest, weak, and obstinate. There is obstinacy in his mouth, or else one reads it there because it is found in his character. St. Peter's was crowded, but only a few people knelt when he came in; every one seemed to regard his coming as a *spectacle*. The person who struck me as having most feeling about the matter was an old woman from the Campagna, who had stationed herself just behind me. I was very satisfactorily placed by the base of a column, which afforded me a good seat; but my old woman was quite resolved that my comfort should not interfere with her view, and when I was about to sit down, she gave such a fierce and audible growl that general attention was attracted to her. Of course I moved—the Pope was much more to her than he was to me, and she had more right to a good position. One thing I admired and envied was the Pope's power of abstraction. With the train of bishops and priests behind him, and the crowd gazing at him, he knelt and repeated his prayers with an air of real devotion, for which I hope I felt all due reverence.

As to his illness, there was a long account in *Galignani* of all that went on in the Sistine Chapel after he fainted; but as we ourselves saw him walk out, though very strangely and hurriedly, and as I believe he fainted afterwards, I presume the account is not strictly true. Then some people said he had been dining with the King of Naples and had eaten too much, and others declared he had been poisoned; all, you see, being the same kind of reports which might have been current in England.

Giuseppe, who is a Florentine, and the most anti-Papal of Italians, gave us the first information on the subject, with a tone and countenance which he vainly endeavoured to make expressive of regret, ending with, "*il risultato non è saputo;*" at which, knowing his secret feelings, I am afraid we were more amused than we ought to have been. The indifference of the people generally, and their want of reverence, are very evident. The Pope passed through the Via Sistina the other day in a carriage, on his way to the Quirinal; a rabble followed, and two or three persons knelt, but that was all. A few mornings ago, Maria, our Italian housemaid, came running in in a state of great excitement, to say that a picture had been found in a little street leading out of the Piazza del Popolo, representing the Pope with two knives stuck in his throat, and underneath written "*un poco piu e poi è finito.*" The picture was coloured or draped with black, and the arms of Victor Emmanuel were over it. The people were crowding to see it, and in a state of rejoicing, because a gendarme had just passed without noticing it. Of course it was taken down immediately, but, like other things of the same kind, I suppose it did its work. Being at Rome is, in fact, like living above a moral and political earthquake; the rumbling reaches us from time to time, and there are plain indications of what is going on beneath; but we do not seem at all likely to arrive at the end desired by so many—an outbreak, and the entrance of Victor Emmanuel. Tricolour flags are indeed set up by unknown persons on inaccessible places; and we are told of tricolour preparations for the entrance of the Sardinians; and all kinds of curious little ways of cheating the police, and showing the tricolour in a manner which cannot be taken notice of. Some of the women wear the colours under their dress. The Government are most watchful, and absurdly suspicious. A young lady told me that she was walking through the streets one day, holding in her hand two or three flowers which happened to be of the forbidden hues, and she found herself followed by one of the Carabinieri for some distance. The people, I hear, sometimes venture to cry "*Viva il Rè*," even in the Pope's presence; but so long as the French troops are here, what good will that do?

There was an illumination the other day in remembrance—some said of the Pope's return from Gaeta in 1848;—others, of his miraculous deliverance when the floor of a building on which he was standing fell in: anyhow, there was an illumination, but all was done according to order. The police went round and told the people they must illuminate, or they would be punished. Some young men in a college put out several lights, and the police carried off six to prison. The Pope evidently feels that his day is come, for he allows printed sonnets to be pasted up at the door of St. Peter's, praising himself, and warning the people that, although the wicked tricolour may flourish for a time, the hour of vengeance from Heaven will surely arrive. Victor Emmanuel is denounced by name, and Louis Napoleon by implication. The people are very ingenious in their political contrivances. The other night there was an expectation of a demonstration; the gendarmes patrolled the Corso, but found no one. The next morning the streets were strewn with pieces of paper, marked, "*Viva il nostro Re, Vittorio Emmanuele!*" which the police had the pleasure of picking up: writers of course unknown.

We have glimpses of the Neapolitan royal family occasionally. I feel sorry for the pretty little Princesses when I see them, but one's pity can go no further. They had a balcony near the place where we were stationed, in the Piazza del Popolo, the other night, when there were grand illuminations— the "Girandola," as it is called— on the Pincian. The Queen came forward every now and then, and her countenance struck me as pleasing, refined, and intellectual. The King too was there, but I only saw him for an instant, as he got out of his carriage and walked through the lines of French bayonets, which were present, as they are everywhere, to preserve peace. The Quirinal is their palace, and in consequence no one is allowed to see more than the gardens, which command a fine view over Rome, and have long walks, and flower-beds, and water-works, throwing up jets in the most unexpected manner, and giving you the opportunity of getting wet through without a moment's notice. Yet, after all, it is but a small enclosure for royalty. The Pope, I was told, rides his mule up and down the walks when he resides there; and the Queen of Naples exercises her horse in a similar way,—but I should think she must sigh for the Bay of Naples.

The Neapolitan family appear devout, and so far give a good example to the people, about whose religious feeling I am really not competent to form an opinion. Mr. —— thinks there will be a terrible rush of infidelity when the present pressure is removed; but I cannot help hoping for better things. The churches are neglected when compared with what they are in other parts of the Continent. There are apparently very few services, and very few worshippers; but then I suspect a good deal in the way of worship goes on when we are not there to see, I mean at an early hour. It is said that a strict watch is kept to prevent any one from going to the English Church. An Italian gentleman told Mr. —— that he longed to go, but did not dare. Police are always stationed by the door of the English Church to keep order amongst the carriages, and of course they would take notice of any Italian who entered. An Italian catechism, published some years ago, has lately been reprinted, in which the people are warned against the insidious heresies of Protestantism generally, and of the English particularly. The lies it contains send one into fits of laughter. Amongst other things, it says that you may know the English by their always carrying a Bible or Prayer-book under their arm; by which we suppose is meant the red "Murray," which every English person travels with. Luther began the Reformation because he was angry that the Pope did not grant the sale of indulgences to his Order. He, and Calvin, and Melancthon, and, in fact, all the Reformers, died the most horrible deaths, &c. &c.

What can one expect from a people brought up upon such falsehoods? But I question whether the ignorance is confined to the lower orders. I have heard an anecdote from most excellent authority, of a "Monsignore," who in the course of conversation quoted a well-known saying from a Latin poet, prefacing it with—"As St. Paul says in the Epistle to the Romans." Seeing that his hearer looked astonished, he added, "It is in the Epistle to the Romans, surely; or if it is not, St. Augustine says it is!" Yours, &c. &c.

I am tempted to give a few more extracts from that most truth-telling Italian catechism,* for the book is not likely to be widely circulated in England, and it really is a remarkable specimen of what in these days of steam vessels, railways, and general civilization, our neighbours on the Continent think and believe about us.

* Catechismi intorno al Protestantesimo ed alla Chiesa Cattolica, per Giovanni Perrone. Roma Stab. Tipog. Aurelj. E. C., 1861.

"*Q.* What are the marks by which foreign propagators of Protestantism may be discerned?*

"*A.* With regard to the English, who are like birds of prey, spreading themselves everywhere for the sake of what they can get, their signs are the following:—At the beginning they make themselves out to be very devout and religious; they practise the outward exercises of their worship very carefully; they have always their Bible or their Prayer-book, as they call it, under their arm; they observe Sunday with a pharisaical superstition. Wherever they have chapels they attend in great numbers, and with much pomp, in order to have an imposing appearance. They contrive to pass for persons of honour and probity, and having thus prepared the way, and predisposed, while yet at a distance, those whom they wish to take captive, they insinuate themselves into families, into general society, and public assemblies, and thus form friendships with those whom they discover are likely to be taken in. Then they commence by compassionating the poor Catholics, slaves of the Pope and the priests, and bound in the trammels of superstition. They exalt to the skies their own free religion, in which there are no fasts, no abstinences, no confessions, nor any of the like oppressive observances. They

* Lezione IX.

" laud the extent of their commerce, the happiness
" and prosperity at which England has arrived,
" now that it has thrown off the Papal yoke. The
" great dunces, (*goccioloni,*) who know no better,
" hear with amazement all these fine tales; they
" admire, and, by degrees, they allow themselves
" to be caught in the toils of these expert hunters.

" *Q.* Why do you call those who admire the
" fine things they hear from the English, dunces?

" *A.* Because they allow themselves to believe
" what is said by these ridiculous charlatans in
" their chatterings; and accepting the appearance,
" do not inquire into the substance.

" *Q.* Explain yourself better; what do you mean
" by the appearance?

" *A.* The appearance is that outside show, which
" is seen in them as in the Pharisees, who showed
" themselves most rigid in the observance of the
" Sabbath, most attentive to the external rites of
" the Jewish worship, most exact in paying tithes;
" but within were proud as Lucifer, avaricious as
" Judas, rapacious, impure, envious, so that the
" Divine Saviour called them a generation of vipers,
" and whitened sepulchres. Such are these here-
" tics, these English proselytisers, whose work really
" is only that of political emissaries, seeking every-
" where influence and preponderance.

" *Q.* What do you mean by substance?

"*A.* By substance, I mean that which Protes-
"tantism, apart from these fine words, truly is in
"England, whether in regard to religion, morality,
"or worldly prosperity. In religion there is a
"chaos and confusion of ideas, which it would be
"impossible to describe. There are hundreds of
"sects fighting like combatants in the lists. The
"Church established—that is to say, supported by
"Government, and of which the King or Queen is
"the head—knows neither what it believes, nor
"what it disbelieves. The so-called Bishops are
"such vile slaves, that they fatten upon the enor-
"mous incomes paid them by the Government.
"Ecclesiastical Benefices are set up for sale to the
"highest bidder, and the newspapers take care to
"advertise that with such a living there will be
"very little to do, and with such another many
"advantages to be gained. The Thirty-nine Arti-
"cles of their creed are so elastic, that every one
"can understand them in his own sense, however
"opposite may be the interpretations. Then as to
"morality, Protestants, taken generally, are the
"most addicted of all persons to sensual pleasures,
"robberies, murder, and suicides, as may be seen
"by their statistics. And with regard to the pros-
"perity of England, take away the few rich persons
"who have colossal fortunes, and the people will
"be found to be groaning under a pauperism so

"deplorable, that in order to escape death from
"starvation they are willing to pass the greater
"part of their days in deep coal mines, or in factories,
"where they die in a few years. And with all this,
"it still happens every year, both in England and
"Ireland, that some thousands die of hunger, or,
"if they wish to escape this misery, emigrate by
"hundreds and thousands, and drag their wretched-
"ness to the distant countries of the American con-
"tinent, or elsewhere. What do you think of such
"happiness as this?

"*Q.* Indeed, I should never have believed it.
"But is what you have told me quite true?

"*A.* In all which I have said there is not a tittle
"beyond the truth; I speak of facts public and
"notorious, and of which whoever has been for
"some time in England must have a personal
"experience.

"And to tell you a few things more in detail,
"you must know that within the last few years it
"has been reckoned that there are in London
"twelve thousand children educated in crime, thirty
"thousand thieves, six thousand receivers of stolen
"goods, twenty-three thousand drunkards, and two
"hundred and twenty thousand leading a life of
"shame. To this may be added infanticide, which
"may almost be called common in England amongst
"the poor, who are instigated to it by the hope of

"gaining a few pence. In Leeds, in one single
"year, there were numbered three hundred of these
"innocent victims. And then, such is the misery
"in Ireland, that, in 1856, more than twenty-one
"thousand, according to the most moderate calcu-
"lation, died of hunger alone. But to sum up the
"whole, I will conclude this sad picture in the
"words of a very recent writer, who, after sixteen
"years' residence and observation in England, thus
"expresses himself:—

"'If we put together all the evils of every
"description which may be found amongst Catholic
"nations, who number more than one hundred and
"fifty (or more strictly speaking two hundred) mil-
"lions of souls, the whole would not equal that of
"which I have just endeavoured to give a sketch.'
"And that we may form some idea of the felicity
"of the English, a Protestant author shows that if,
"during the last century, the population of England
"has trebled, the number of the poor has at the
"same time increased eight-fold in proportion.
"Such is the happiness of which the supporters of
"Protestantism wish to make Italy a sharer!

"*Q.* God preserve us from it!"

Who will not devoutly echo the prayer? Yet amidst the monstrous mis-statements, and false inferences to be found in the foregoing extracts, there is undoubtedly much to make an English person, most especially a member of the English Church, very sad. Truth and falsehood are so ingeniously mingled together, that it would be a hopeless task to separate them. The whole is indeed a most remarkable instance of the talent for misrepresentation, or drawing from isolated facts deductions according to preconceived impressions, which is so fatally common both with nations and individuals. The author gives in his preface what he evidently considers a convincing proof of the truth of his accusation. Within the last seven years, his catechism has, he says, passed through twenty editions; ten thousand copies have been circulated in Rome alone, and eighteen thousand in the Milanese; not to mention two French editions, two German, and one Spanish: yet no one has yet had the courage to contradict its assertions. Strange it seems, that the nation against whom the chief charges are brought should be the only one which has not had the benefit of hearing them!

But doubtless all is best as it is. I question myself whether any one in England would ever take the trouble to expose such a tissue of falsehoods and fallacies; and unless this were done, the author of the Italian catechism would only be the more thoroughly convinced of the incontrovertible character of his statements. He would not be likely to understand that where there is an evident wish to distort facts, and to believe ill, the silence with which assertions are received proves not that their truth is acknowledged, but that they show a spirit of unfairness, which renders it useless to attempt their refutation.

CHAPTER XV.

46, Via Sistina, April 17th, 1861.

My dear ——,

I am wishing to write to you whenever I see anything pleasant or interesting, and that is continually. But time, as you will understand, runs very short. We have had but indifferent weather lately—much more rain than is usual at this season in Rome; and this has interfered with some country excursions, which are now all being crowded together, for we have only three weeks more to condense them into. Yesterday we managed an enchanting expedition to Ostia, which has been talked of ever since we came to Rome. We had a drive of fifteen miles over the Campagna first, then an exploration of some excavations in the old town of Ostia, and lastly a picnic in the pine woods of Castel Fusano. We started before eight, and were not home till nearly seven in the evening. It was a glorious day—such sunshine and blue sky as are only to be seen in Italy; and besides—what I never expected to find here—the most brilliant, delicate green foliage which one could desire for a finished picture. I don't know whether it is the beauty of the early spring only, but certainly the pencilling of the young leaves, especially when they are seen in contrast with the dark pines, is singularly beautiful. After crossing the Campagna we had lanes and woods as we might have had in England, and then came out upon some salt marshes, which need no description beyond the name. Modern Ostia is close to them, and a most dreary place it is. Even to look at it would be enough to tell one that it was haunted by malaria; yet Julius the Second built a castle there, which stands up grandly at the present day. I wonder how he managed to baffle malaria. That is one of the most perplexing of all Roman problems, and it meets one at every turn. Ancient Ostia was about a mile from the modern town. We had Signor Visconti, the Pope's chief excavator, to show us what has been done in the way of discovery; and I followed him closely, and gave all my attention to his explanations, and really gained a fair idea of the whole thing.

The ground-plan of the town has been brought to light after being hidden for centuries, and one can walk over the mosaic pavements, and along the principal street, with the marks of the chariot wheels still traceable, and go in and out of an old Roman house, as easily as in England we could walk over the foundations of one in process of building. The houses must have been very small, and the streets very narrow, but most remarkable of all is the size of the temples; they must have been mere nutshells compared with our churches. The Baths and Circus were infinitely more important. The mosaic pavement of the former is wonderfully preserved. Water seems to have been prized in ancient times much more than it is now—witness the fountains in Rome, and there are evident remains of some at Ostia. We wandered about, and stood, and examined—all under a very hot sun— till I was in no slight degree weary, and then we went on still farther towards the old stone walls said to be the remains of an ancient port and quay dating from the founder of Ostia, Ancus Martius, —if it is allowable to believe that such an individual ever lived. Very interesting it was, and if only one could have been permitted to sit and meditate, one might have been worked up to a considerable degree of enthusiasm; but it was rather like looking at the bones from which a comparative anatomist draws out the complete figure of the unknown animal. You required to understand in order to appreciate, and if you could not understand, you were obliged to have recourse to imagination; for the exercise of which the sun at Ostia was too hot, and the road by which we had come too long. My material cravings for *sight* were better satisfied by a large wine cellar, which had been lately uncovered. The enormous stone casks were sunk deep into the ground, where they must have lain, in all probability, ever since the Saracens destroyed the city in the fifth century.

There is immense interest in all this, but it is not what we in England call beauty. The first thing indeed I should say to a person coming to Rome from England would be a warning against expecting any beauty in the ruins generally, except that of association. Only where the columns of a temple are standing, or where the building has been stone and not brick, can one discover anything like the poetry of time, which makes English decay so marvellously picturesque. Yet I am wrong, too, for wherever green has sprung up amongst the brickwork, or trees have found a place in its vicinity, there is exceeding beauty; but these are the exceptions rather than the rule.

The amount of beauty to be found in the outline of massiveness is not understood until the thin layers of Roman bricks, cemented together till they become one, are compared with the rough but homogeneous surface of a block of limestone. The latter also takes colour in so much greater variety than brick. A weather-stained stone wall is a perfect study for an artist; but nothing would make Roman bricks a study for any one except an antiquary. The remains of a Temple of Jupiter were the great attraction at Ostia before the recent excavations were made; but they are a striking illustration of what I have just been saying. For a Temple, the building is large; it is circular in form, and approached by a flight of broad steps; and an altar to the god is still standing in its place. It ought to be a beautiful ruin, but it is not. It ought to bear its age written on its walls, but it does not; cold and bare, it stands apart, as unable to touch human sympathies, as the religion which it was built to uphold. Yet one charm it has; it looks out upon the Campagna and the mountains; —and the Campagna, though drearily desolate in many parts, yet is varied in others by exquisite bits of copsewood; whilst the green grass is always a bright foreground, beyond which the mountains rise so grey and soft, and yet so firm in their outline, and with such ever-changing interest from the light and shade which floats over them, that one can never tire of looking at them. The snow rests on them still; and lately there have been white thunder-clouds floating around them, so that one could not distinguish where the clouds ended and the snow began.

Castel Fusano, where we had our luncheon, is about two miles from Ostia, close to the sea. It is an old, dilapidated, fortified villa of the Chigi family, built in the seventeenth century. It made me think of some of the old manor-houses in England, which have fallen to decay, and been converted into farm-houses. The Chigi family would probably be very indignant if they heard me say so, for it is their villa still; and when not prevented by malaria, I believe they visit it. It is a gaunt old house, more picturesque than the generality of Italian houses, thanks to the pirates, who in days gone by infested the coast, and caused the lords of Castel Fusano, as a matter of defence, to build low towers, with loopholes, at the angles of their mansion. We did not trouble ourselves to see the interior, but collected together at some little distance from the house, under the shade of the pine-trees, and there spread our dinner in true picnic style, with the trunk of a tree for a table; and very pleasant the rest, and refreshment, and coolness were. After dinner I walked down an old Roman paved road, a mile in length, with ilexes, and pines, and lighter trees stretching away on each side, and a profusion of lovely wild flowers,—forget-me-nots, and brilliant pink cyclamens, growing underneath them; and at length came upon the Mediterranean, intensely blue and sparkling. But there was a long reach of sand before I could get quite close to it, and I contented myself with a distant view, and sat down alone on a camp seat, looking at one most perfect little bit of the wood, and thinking of you, and wondering how I should ever make you *feel* the way in which the dark low branches of the ilexes stretched across the old Roman road, and the sunshine danced upon the bank which bordered it, and the young green leaves stood out from the grey shadows of the forest.

One can see such things in England, yet not quite the same, for there are no such ilex woods and pines, and, consequently, no such contrast and yet blending of colours. And then there are the associations. The Villa at Castel Fusano stands on the site of a celebrated villa which belonged to Pliny; and all the interest of the old Roman world, as regarded commerce, had once centred in its neighbourhood. That is a thought which could never be called up in England.

We drove home across the Campagna as the daylight began to fade, but whilst the sunset was still brilliant. So lovely it was!—The mountains soft as fairy-land, and the villages below the Alban Mount standing out quite clear; dark shadows on the low green mounds, the Tiber looking almost blue in the evening light, and Rome in the distance —a long line of misty buildings, with the grey dome of St. Peter's rising in the centre.

Yours, &c. &c.

CHAPTER XVI.

The excavations at Ostia lead naturally to excavations in general, and the Catacombs in particular; and here the same kind of difficulty arises which is felt with regard to so many other subjects in Rome. The Catacombs have been so explored, so discussed, that it is absolutely impossible to say anything new about them. All that can be attempted is a description of the few points in which they created a different impression from that anticipated. The Catacombs are not, as I supposed, one vast burying-place, but many. There are said to be no less than sixty, and since their first formation many have been connected with churches built in honour of some of the Martyrs who have been interred in them. The entrances are to be found in very opposite directions. There are about eight which have been sufficiently opened to be visited, and amongst these a choice can be made. Two of the most important are those of S. Calisto and S. Agnese, and from them an accurate impression may be obtained of all. When we visited S. Calisto we drove out a considerable distance on the Appian Way, lost our road—thanks to a very ignorant coachman—and

only discovered the place of our destination by
seeing a tablet marked " Entrance to the Catacomb
of S. Calisto," placed over a little door in a wall,
opening into a vineyard, by the road-side. The
most simple, rustic, *unsolemn* of sites it appeared.
We had driven along a dusty road, under a bright,
hot sun; all signs of life and earth, busy and ordinary, surrounded us. A small party of friends,
who were engaged to go with us, met us at the
entrance to the vineyard, and we went in and strolled
along the path, talking upon ordinary subjects, till we
came to a little door in a rock. I have seen entrances
to wine cellars very like it. Rather an uncomfortable sensation stole over me then, for we all paused,
and our guide, unlocking the door, struck a light
and gave to each of us a long torch; (I forgot to
say that we had been told to provide ourselves
with torches, and had brought some with us;) he
then led the way into a narrow passage, just wide
enough for one person, and we all followed.

Once within the cavern and the awe became
less, at least for the first five or ten minutes.
Excavations made by man do not, I think, excite
the same feelings as the caverns formed by nature.
Where your fellow-creatures have been, you do not
fear to follow; and the galleries of the Catacombs
are so regular and well-formed, the steps by which
you descend from one tier to the other are for

the most part so safe, that you pass along easily
and naturally, not realizing at first the strangeness
and solemnity of the place in which you find yourself. And it is some time before you lose the impression of the bright upper air which you have
left; it is only as you go on and on, finding no end to
the passages, so narrow and so same, and after two
or three turnings become aware that you could not
retrace your way, that a chill of awe steals over you,
and you look anxiously back to be quite sure that
there is no lingerer behind, and no extinguished
torch. Still I doubt whether the impression which
the Catacombs produce is really so overwhelming
as has sometimes been represented. They bear
the impress of death, but death itself has for the
most part ceased to inhabit them. There are the
long narrow shelves, on which were once laid the
mortal remains of human beings; but the crumbling
dust is, with few exceptions, all that is now to be
seen. Those exceptions indeed give the real,
startling, yet touching history of these caverns.
When you look, as you imagine, upon an empty
tomb, and amidst the mingled sand, and dust, and
fragments of stone, catch a glimpse of a human skull,
or the bones of a crumbling skeleton, you feel what
before you only endeavoured to believe, that human
love and human sorrow have found their rest in
these dark galleries; that the cold hewn walls have

witnessed the end of the sternest tragedies of earth, that you are in a place where laughter would be profanation, and where the blessedness, even of prayer, can have been felt only after the bitter struggle with grief.

But such impressions as these, even when made, cannot be long retained whilst wandering through the Catacombs. They are the very battle-field of controversy, and, strive as you may to escape it, controversy will follow you there. As you pass along the galleries you meet with openings which lead into small recesses, or chambers, generally known as cubicula. These are supposed to have been used for family vaults and places of worship. In some, sarcophagi have been found; in others, there are the ordinary shelves, or loculi, with perhaps an arched space, called an arcosolium, over one grave, marking that the person there deposited was worthy of particular veneration. In these cubicula are to be found the chief remains of the frescoes and inscriptions which have been the source of so much discussion. The examination of them is very interesting, but it destroys anything like feeling. As you stand with a torch in your hand, trying to throw the light upon some faded outline of a figure, which may represent Jonah, or Daniel, or Moses, but which is also so extremely quaint, that an effort is required to resist a sense of the ludicrous, anything like a perception of the deep meaning and importance of the subject is almost unattainable. What you are really trying to understand is, how it is possible that modern Romanism can find anything upon which to build, in remains so slight, so simple, and so devoid of any characteristics, except those which belong alike to all Christians. And if, as was the case with myself, you have the advantage of a companion who has thoroughly explored the Catacombs, and learnt all that is to be known about them from the most careful students of the present day, your chief desire is not so much to examine for yourself, as to listen to all that he is saying, and not to miss any painting or inscription which may throw the least additional light upon the subject of controversy. If you might only be permitted to remain behind, to seat yourself in one of the cubicula, and think, feeling might be very easy; but it would require in a woman strong nerves and a very unimaginative mind to endure that. If you thought at all, or felt at all, you might think and feel a great deal too much, as you watched the glimmering torches dying away at the end of the long gallery, and heard the sound of the retreating footsteps; and then turned to your own torch, liable to be extinguished by a gust of air, or any incautious movement; and looking around you saw the hollow spaces where the dead had lain, and stretching out your hand touched the very dust which, it might be, had once formed a portion of their bodies. It may be better after all to be controversial; there is no fear of too much imagination then. And to a member of the English Church, who has no wish to see what is not to be seen, the examination which controversy requires brings a very satisfactory result. If the Catacombs prove anything of the religious system of primitive Christianity, they prove that we are able to identify ourselves with it without any straining or effort. The frescoes and inscriptions might belong to an English Church; and in no place could the words of mingled sorrow and hope of the English burial-service fall more fitly or soothingly on the ear than in these early Christian resting-places. S. Calisto is probably the largest, and S. Agnese the most interesting of the Catacombs. In the former, however, there are some remains well worthy of note; amongst them the sarcophagus, cut in the wall, in which the body of S. Cecilia was placed after her martyrdom; and where it was subsequently found, lying in the attitude so touchingly represented in her church in the Trastevere, to which it was removed by Paschal the Second. Cornelius, Bishop of Rome, the contemporary of S. Cyprian of Carthage, was also buried in the Catacomb of S.

Calisto. He was martyred at Civita Vecchia, and his remains were deposited in a wide grave forming one side of a square chamber. The tomb was used, as was so frequently the custom, for an altar; and before it is a short pillar, on which formerly stood a lamp, continually kept burning. Rough paintings of Cornelius and Cyprian are sketched on the side walls. The Bishop of Rome owed the public acknowledgment of his valid election to the decision of the Bishop of Carthage; and though Cyprian was martyred in Africa, yet the memories of both were preserved in the one festival.

The burning lamps must have been commonly used, from the number which have been found in the excavations, but which are becoming more and more rare; many said to be ancient being, in fact, manufactured. They were doubtless used reverentially, but they must also have been necessary; the only light admitted into the Catacombs being obtained by occasional vertical shafts. The inscriptions most common in the Catacombs are a name, and a date of months and days; and the words "*In pace*" are often carefully engraved, but as often scratched roughly upon the stone. There are some inscriptions of greater length attributed to Pope Damasus, who died A.D. 324. I mention them because where everything is so vague it is a pleasure to seize upon something which tells its tale almost without explanation. Pope Damasus took immense interest in the Catacombs, and set up numerous inscriptions, which can be recognised at once by the large clear letters, cut apparently with the express object of baffling the mouldering, defacing effects of time. One of these, in a cubiculum near the entrance of the S. Calisto Catacomb, gives the names of the Bishops of Rome who were buried there, ending with a wish to be laid near them himself, though he dared not aspire to such an honour. A similar wish has been carried out frequently. In several of the Arcisolia, where the remains of martyrs were deposited, the frescoes have been cut through in order that a loculus may be opened close to the spot so reverenced. The size of the loculi varies of course; occasionally in the galleries you come upon numbers of children's graves, close together; some so small, that the little ones could scarcely have entered into this lower life before they were transplanted to a higher.

The particular interest of the Catacombs of S. Agnese lies in the fact that they are connected with the sandpits or arenariæ, from which the volcanic ashes, called Pozzolana, used in the composition of Roman mortar, can be obtained. It was once supposed that these arenariæ were converted by the early Christians into Catacombs; but a careful inspection proves that this could not possibly have been the case. We went into them ourselves. They were like any other extensive sandpits,—low, vaulted, and irregular; whereas the Catacombs are even and narrow, and though actually excavations, yet look almost like galleries formed by walls built up expressly for the purpose. The arenariæ might have been, and probably were, however, used as entrances to the Catacombs. At S. Agnese a stair leads from them into the galleries and to a deep shaft, by which the bodies of the dead were, it is supposed, lowered to their burying-place.

Other and very interesting Catacombs have lately been opened in connexion with the Church of S. Alessandro, recently uncovered, after lying buried for centuries under the accumulated soil of the Campagna. They had been but little disturbed when we saw them. Many of the grave-shelves were still closed by the slabs of marble, bearing rough inscriptions, which were inserted when first the dead were deposited there; and in one case we saw a little Christian lamp encased in the tufa which enclosed the resting-place of a martyr,—a space being left for the vase which contained his blood. It was the custom to seal the grave with a stamp, inscribed "*Spes in Deo.*"

Several of these stamps have been found, and are now kept in the Vatican Museum; but the impression made on the mortar or cement must long since have been obliterated.

There are many very curious tombs, and chambers, and frescoes, in the S. Agnese Catacombs, but in one respect they are disappointing. Instead of carrying the mind back to the very beginning of Christianity, they rather carry it forward several centuries. You cannot believe that in the first days of persecution, when the Christians were so few in number, there could have been leisure for so much even rough ornament and sculpture; and the fifth, or even the fourth century, to which you are compelled to attribute a great deal which you see, seems modern; and you are instinctively suspicious of corruption and superstition. This is a fact which it is desirable fully to realize before visiting the Catacombs. To expect too much is of course to enjoy too little. The most ancient of the Catacombs is, I believe, that of S. Nereo e Achilleo, which is said to date from the reign of Vespasian. This I did not see, but it could have contained very few inscriptions, as there are not above one or two of the first century to be found amongst those which have been placed in the Vatican and Lateran Museums. What use the

Christians of the third, fourth, and fifth centuries made of the Catacombs—how they assembled to celebrate the Eucharist over the tombs of the martyrs, and met in the cubicula for the purpose probably of instructing the catechumens—may be discovered from the altar-tombs and rough chairs, which are hewn out of the rock that forms the walls of the little chambers. But what was done before that period must, for the most part, be matter for conjecture; and I think that if I had been prepared for this previously to seeing the Catacombs, I should have been more willing to accept thankfully all I found there, without wishing, as I certainly did, for something additional.

The effect of oppression and awfulness which the Catacombs produce on the mind is only thoroughly understood upon emerging from them. When you again breathe the free air, and look up into the sky, you seem to have passed through an actual resurrection; and the outer world, so familiar in its freshness and beauty, is gifted with a newer and more invigorating power of life and enjoyment, in contrast with the dark yet peaceful regions below. For they are indescribably peaceful; that is one very singular effect produced by them. And yet not singular. If the spirit which pervades the material scenes beheld upon the earth, or under the earth, is that which affects the mind, the Catacombs, as they are amongst the most solemn and subduing, so also must they be amongst the most calm and hopeful of localities. The very gloom which pervades them makes the faith which consecrates them stronger and more clear. I remember thinking as I passed through them what it would be to bring there any who had been dearly loved, and the thought caused a momentary shudder; but it could not last. Rough as the records in the Catacombs are, they tell of a personal realization of Christian hope for which one might well exchange all the brightness which earth can give. And it is this nearness to the unseen world, this presence of paradise, which is the abiding impression that lingers on the mind after visiting them. I saw the Catacombs of S. Calisto on the Monday in Holy Week, and felt that they were only one degree less suited to the season than the services of the Church.

Years ago, I recollect seeing another burial-place—a Catacomb also. It was in Paris, when the present Church of St. Genevieve was the Pantheon—the desecrated church standing in the centre of Paris, and bearing on its front the proud inscription, "*Aux grands hommes, la Patrie reconnaissante.*" On entering the building we crossed a large bare hall,—formerly the body of the church, but then containing only the statue of Immortality, with golden rays encircling her head,—and descended into the vaulted crypt. The cold stone passages, extending in every direction, were dimly seen in the glimmering light. There were monuments all round; and that which first caught the eye was the ghastly statue of a man, with a singularly thin, sharp, mocking countenance. It was Voltaire. Rousseau was close to him. Our guide lighted a torch, and led us aside into a narrow passage, and turning his face against the wall shouted loudly, and all through the arches the echo rolled and thundered; and then he spoke and laughed, and again the echo was fearfully distinct. In that unhallowed place there was no reverence for the dead.

We hurried away; but the effect produced I have never forgotten. As we came out into the open bustling streets, there was a heavy weight upon my mind, for which I felt that the only relief would be to enter a church, if but for a few moments. People may perhaps call that feeling superstition, but "there are more things in heaven and earth than are dreamt of in our philosophy."

CHAPTER XVII.

AFTER the Catacombs, heathen relics and excavations are comparatively unexciting, yet one cannot long be in Rome without desiring to know everything that is to be learnt about them. The process of excavation is going on continually, being sometimes undertaken by Government, and sometimes by persons of private enterprise. When we were in Rome, Cavaliere Guidi was making some remarkable explorations, on the site of the Villa and Gardens which Cæsar left to the people by his will. There were others going on near the railway-works by the Baths of Domitian, and others again some miles out of Rome on the Campagna.

The treasures discovered are either placed in the public Museums, or kept for sale by the private excavators, who are in this way alone repaid for their labour and risk, and therefore keep a strict watch over the purloining practices of visitors. I observed as we were going over Cæsar's Villa, that whenever any of us lingered behind there was a quick glance to see what we were doing. The Pope's excavator at Ostia was naturally more liberal, and when asked by one of our party whether she might carry away a piece of marble with some letters cut upon it, only smiled, and begged that his permission might not be required.

Cæsar's Villa, which is near the Porta Portese on the road to Civita Vecchia, is very extensive. Some magnificent mosaic pavements have already been laid open, and every day throws more light upon the extent of the buildings which were included under the name. I can imagine, that after a time excavating would become a perfect passion. There must be the study beforehand, the thorough comprehension of the locality, and then the search— almost sure to bring the reward of success. It is most tantalizing though to know what treasures lie hidden under modern Rome, which there does not appear to be the least probability of obtaining. I was told that when the columns of Trajan's Forum were laid open, now many years ago, the Roman Government took fright at the rate at which the work of excavation proceeded, and built the two hideous churches which now on one side cover the ground, in order to prevent its being continued. The present Government gives certainly much more encouragement to such labours; but Cavaliere Guidi carries on a great deal at his own expense. We visited with him the Church of S. Alessandro, about six miles out of Rome, on the Campagna, and now in process of excavation; and he described to us how he had found it.

From the history of the Martyrs it was known that Pope Alexander the First, who suffered martyrdom in the reign of Trajan, A.D. 117, had been buried seven miles out of Rome, in a cemetery belonging to a Roman lady converted to Christianity. A presbyter and a deacon had also, it was said, been buried at the same place with him; and there was the tradition of a Church having been built over their graves. Cavaliere Guidi knew all this, and he commenced his search in the locality which he thought most likely to be the true one. After a time he discovered in a field a stone with a heathen inscription. The early Christians were, as he was well aware, in the habit of taking stones of this kind for their buildings; and having such an indication, he began his work and dug in that spot. As he went lower and lower signs of the Church became visible, and now it is all open: the vestibule, an oratory paved with fragments of marble, and the central portion of the church, containing the altar, supported by four roughly-worked pillars, and having underneath it the sarcophagus, in which the bodies of the martyrs were deposited when the church was built; whilst behind is a kind of apse with a bishop's seat—a stone chair of rude workmanship. Other little chambers there are adjoining the central building, one, which forms a kind of second church, having been, it is supposed, appropriated for catechumens or women. The Catacombs connected with the Church, and to which I have before referred, have also been opened, and are supposed to be of considerable extent.

S. Stefano is another Church on the Campagna which has been lately uncovered. It is even more perfect and interesting than S. Alessandro, and dates (so we were told by a priest who was visiting the excavations, and was in attendance upon a Bishop) from 590. It was destroyed in the twelfth century. The plan of the early Christian churches, with the closed choir and tribune, is clearly shown in it; and there are Catacombs seven tier deep, but not sufficiently excavated to be easily entered.

Heathenism puts forth its rival claims to attention now, as it did in the first days of Christianity. The ruins of both lie side by side; and turning from the Church of S. Stefano, a stranger may see, at the distance of a few yards, the openings which lead to two wonderful Roman tombs, of the age of Marcus Aurelius. They also are a recent discovery, and can be seen only by torch-light. Exquisitely ornamented they are, with arabesque patterns in fresco and stucco; and in an outer chamber connected with one of them are two heads in bas-relief, representing, as it would seem, husband and wife. But there is something more tangible than art to connect that long past age with the present, for in the sarcophagus which stands in the centre of the inner chamber are two skulls, the actual relics of the human beings whose earthly love, and joy, and sorrow, found there an unbroken rest.

The labour and art bestowed upon these sepulchral monuments is strange and striking. The heathen were braver than ourselves, or else they feared so much, that in very despair they were driven to defiance. Death—grand, adorned—inviting, even commanding admiration and inspection, meets you everywhere in Rome. The Castle of S. Angelo is but the vast mausoleum, in the centre of which is the sepulchral chamber built to contain the ashes of Hadrian. The round tower of Cecilia Mettalla, the great landmark of the Campagna, is but one grand tomb amongst the long line of funereal monuments which once bordered the Appian Way, and which may still be traced by the fragments of ruined brickwork, covered with half-defaced inscriptions that have within a few years been uncovered; and closely adjoining the grass-covered graves and grey stones of the lovely Protestant burial-ground, rises, to the height of more than one hundred feet, the great pyramidal tomb of Caius Cestius. In that place especially one could almost be indignant at this asserted superiority,—this claim to mock at death. Yet only until looking upward. Give us the blue sky, and the glad hope of which it tells, and we may be well content to leave hewn stones, and marble, and paintings, to those who had nought else to make death tolerable.

But heathens were not always buried so magnificently. The Columbaria were, like the Catacombs, merely excavated chambers, in which the ashes of the dead, collected in sepulchral urns, were placed in small recesses like pigeon-holes. They appear to have been generally intended for the household servants of some noble family; the bodies of the slaves being thrown in heaps into pits dug near the sepulchres of their masters. I saw one Columbarium in the grounds of the Villa Pamphili Doria, and another on the Appian Way near the Tombs of the Scipios. They gave me a strange and very uncomfortable feeling, as though human weakness had, in its hopeless ignorance and terror, been striving to attain annihilation. One felt there could be no reverence, no feeling connected with them; they were the embodiment of "nothingness."

The Tombs of the Scipios were different. The dark vaulted rocky chambers contain several recesses, in one of which was found the celebrated Sarcophagus of Scipio Barbatus, now in the Vatican, and copies of which are so common; and as the great patrician families of Rome appear to have retained the custom of burying entire until the time of the first Cæsars, we may believe that the bodies, not the burnt ashes of the dead, were deposited here.

It was awful, and scarcely seemed real, to find oneself creeping along the low excavated passages following an old woman, who preceded us with a lighted torch, and stopping to remark inscriptions which told of names so far back and so entirely historical; and to me the tombs of the dead Scipios gave to the actual men a more real life than any that could have been bestowed by volumes recording their deeds. Yet after all one instinctively turns from the mockery of sarcophagi, monuments, and mausoleums, whether heathen or Christian: at the best they are but " whitened sepulchres." To enter the tomb of Caius Cestius, and look round upon the damp walls, was more oppressive far than to stand by the narrow graves, upon which the flowers of Spring were blossoming, in the adjacent Protestant burial-ground.

For it is there that in Rome the thought of death most naturally carries the mind of an English traveller. Guarded by the grand old walls of the city, and joining the green meadows dotted with trees below Monte Testaccio, it might be the brightest, most hope-inspiring resting-place which affection could desire. That it is not so must be attributed chiefly to the thoughts of exile which it awakens; but somewhat of its sadness is doubtless also due to the mournful associations of the two graves to which every English traveller naturally turns.

So much of painful admiration has been bestowed upon Shelley, so much of generous compassion upon Keats, that the judgment pronounced upon them by any one individual can be of no importance. To the world in general " their names can never be writ in water." The grave of Shelley is overgrown and uncared-for—we found it with difficulty. Keats sleeps in the old cemetery, which is at a little distance from the new ground. The spot is more sunny than that assigned to Shelley, and nearer, as it were, to the thoughts, and hopes, and cares of the living; and the old man who had the charge of the cemetery led us thither at once, as well knowing that the steps of an English person would naturally turn to the grave of the young poet who lived too long for his own happiness, though long enough for fame.

CHAPTER XVIII.

46, *Via Sistina, April* ——, 1861.

My dear ——,

If I had written a few days ago, I should have raved about chestnut woods and blue lakes; for I had just returned from a visit to Albano and Frascati. I may write more quietly now, but you will have the advantage of more details. We have been *threatening* Albano for weeks, but the weather has always been against us. As it was, we had a wet morning; that is, it was moderately fine when we set off, and came on to rain before we reached Albano. We started early—only our own party. Of course, our road lay across the Campagna, which is to Rome what the sea is to an island; and our destination was before us the whole way, for Albano is only about twelve miles from Rome, and though the town is not to be seen till you approach near it, yet Monte Cavo, which rises above it, is. One might easily make a classical pilgrimage of nearly every step of the way, but I can never stop to look at details in crossing the Campagna; the distant views, and the scattered bits of ruin in the foreground, are so attractive. Albano stands high, and we ought to have had fine views going up to it, only, thanks to the rain, we had not. It is a country town of the better class. There are some decent houses, and a very respectable hotel, at which, when the rain poured down, we made ourselves tolerably comfortable by the aid of a fire and books. Not very promising for our main object; and as we arrived at mid-day, we had, as people say, the whole afternoon before us. Happily, however, the clouds cleared whilst we were at dinner, and then we ordered donkeys, and set off to see all that could be seen in the course of a few hours.

The thing which tries me most in all these expeditions is not to be able to stop and get up *feeling*. Imagine passing the tomb of Aruns, the son of Porsenna, and not being at all sure whether it is not the monument to the Horatii and Curiatii; and spending the few seconds which the donkey-men allow you in trying to make out what Murray means; studying him seated upon the back of an obstinate animal, who will go in one direction just when you wish to go in another. It is quite absurd to attempt classical ecstatics under such circumstances, and I always find that, except at rare and quiet moments, my feelings are more quickly touched by natural beauty. There is quite enough of that at Albano, and one enjoys it all the more from its being such a strange and unexpected contrast to Rome. Did you ever imagine that the old Romans knew anything about chestnut woods and grey rocks, or that Roman children ever gathered pink cyclamens and blue forget-me-nots? But of course they did, and the Latin children before them. This country about Albano, and in fact all the neighbourhood of the mountains, is so un-Roman, so picturesque and luxuriant, that it is necessary to recall continually where and what it is, in order to establish in the mind the fact that one is not dreaming.

Our donkeys carried us first along a splendid viaduct, of about a mile in length, built over a deep-wooded ravine, which separates Ariccia from Albano. It is a work of Pius the Ninth, and the world may well be grateful to him for it, for a more lovely or more easy ride there cannot be; the arches of the viaduct telling grandly as the road turns, whilst you look down over the trees clothing the hill-side to the stretch of the Campagna. Then, passing beyond Ariccia, you reach Gensano and the Lake of Nemi; the former a wretched Italian town, the latter a lovely little Italian lake—deep blue in a setting of chestnut woods—and far away the smiling, treacherous Mediterranean, with the misty promontory of the Isola San Felice.

We returned by the same road to Albano, and then started in the opposite direction to the Lake of Albano, and Castel Gandolfo, where the Pope has a palace. Of course we had first to mount a steep hill, our donkeys scrambling up a dirty *pavé* street; that is the introduction to all country pleasures in this part of the world. And I might almost say, of course there was a Capuchin convent at the top; for these very un-clean monks have as much taste for beauty as they have for dirt, which is saying a great deal, and delight to look at water, though they object to making use of it. Their convent looks down upon the Lake of Albano, shut in by woods, with Monte Cavo towering above them to the south; whilst on the north-west side the town of Castel Gandolfo, built on a steep narrow ridge, rises perpendicularly above the lake to a height of 460 feet. The Pope's palace is a distinguished object, from its size—beauty it has none. Then, besides—the Capuchin monks have the advantage of being so high that they can see over Castel Gandolfo to the Campagna, and can catch the line of white dots marking where Rome lies. Soracte too is visible, and a long line of hills stretching nearly from the "wave-like" mountain to the Mediterranean; not so grand and beautiful indeed as the Sabine range, but by no means to be despised as the boundary of an extensive landscape. We had but a short time for the view, exquisite though it was; there was so much to be done besides, and every portion of the road was lovely. We rode through what are called galleries all the way to Castel Gandolfo—not galleries hewn in rock, but formed by splendid over-arching ilexes; and when we reached the town went at once to the Barberini Palace, built on the site of Domitian's Villa. The King of Naples is said to have desired it for a summer residence, and he could wish for nothing better, at least as regards the situation. I was haunted by the spectre of Domitian all the time we were there. The extreme beauty of the site, and the extreme wickedness of the man, were in such marked contrast. The gardens are desolate and untidy, and a regiment of Scotch gardeners would be required to put them in order; but I did not long for them, they would have been unsuited to the place. There is a modern house indeed which one would not object to see in order, but to touch the ilex avenues would be profanation; and the broad terraces are better as they are, left to the raggedness of nature, than they would be if trimmed by art. They have a charm which nothing can take from them—the view over the broken foreground of olives, chestnuts, and cottages, to the open plain and the blue sea; and if anything could have touched the imagination, and so possibly softened the heart of such a monster as Domitian, one would think it might have been a view like that. I wonder whether he ever *felt* that it was lovely; if he did, that would have been the time to petition for mercy,—for no one surely could *feel* natural beauty, and then go and sin against the spirit of nature. This sounds rather pantheistic, but what I mean is, that I question whether at the very moment when a person is under the influence of such a view as that from the terraces of Domitian's Villa, he could order half a dozen heads to be cut off. The stables must have been enormous; one of the terraces is built above them. Large masses of the old palace are also left, half hidden with ivy and shrubs. One arch I saw, so old, that a huge tree had embraced it and formed its roof. We had a most perfect ride back to the town, through an ilex gallery, not the same by which we had come, but another skirting the opposite side of the ridge, and close under the ruins of the palace. The Campagna was deep purple, the sky unutterably golden, and we looked upon it through a framework of dark spreading branches and knotted trunks, in one place supported by the fallen columns which must once have formed a portion of the imperial abode.

We went to bed early, for M—— and I were to start the next morning at seven, with Giuseppe and two guides, and go to the top of Monte Cavo.

The rest of the party were to drive to Frascati, where we were to meet them in the middle of the day.

You will be tired of blue lakes and chestnut woods, so I will say as little as I can about them; but though I may forget many pleasures in life, I am not likely to forget the extreme enjoyment of that first early ride round the Alban Lake. The weather was delicious, not in the least too hot or too cold. We set off as on the previous evening, by the Capuchin convent, and then took a winding path along the side of the hill, amongst rocks and trees, exactly in the opposite direction to Castel Gandolfo—the lake being immediately below us. The same un-Roman-like feeling which I mentioned before, was present with me all the time. The site of Alba Longa must have been close at hand; but to associate the rough little town of one's imagination with the scenery around was impossible,—the fact being, I suppose, that nature is always refined, whilst human society is in its beginnings always rude; and to place the two, in thought, in juxtaposition is therefore difficult. We rode half round the lake before we came to Palazzuola, a Franciscan monastery—which was once the site of Alba Longa, then was not, and now seems likely to be so again—all according to antiquaries, who, however, allow that the city could scarcely have stood exactly where the monastery stands, but only near it. Certainly it is very difficult to comprehend how anything approaching to the dignity of a town could have been built on such a ledge. The Franciscan convent is shut in by high walls, and there is only sufficient space for a donkey path between them and the precipitous descent to the lake. There are all kinds of classical reminiscences, and some few remains, in the vicinity. What I should have liked chiefly to have seen would have been the entrance to the subterranean canal, or Emissary, by which the Romans lowered the waters of the Alban Lake when they were carrying on the siege of Veii. But that was at some distance; much nearer, in fact, to Castel Gandolfo. Beyond Palazzuola we turned away from the lake, and went on through the chestnut woods to Rocca di Papa; and when I say woods, I mean also all the adjuncts which make woods beautiful;—the gay colours of exquisite flowers, blue-bells, forget-me-nots, pink cyclamens, and bright yellow broom, in most lavish profusion,—with grey rocks, moss-grown and weather-tinted, peeping out amidst the young green leaves. So much for nature. Then came man's dwellings, in the form of Rocca di Papa, an Italian stable-yard—I beg its pardon, but the street is nothing else—with a few good-sized houses, tenanted, when heat and malaria send the inhabitants of Rome to search for health amongst the hills. A very pleasant summer place I have heard it is; and if one could mount a donkey at one's door, and shut one's eyes whilst passing through the village, I can easily believe it would be so. A donkey must be indispensable; nothing else would clamber up the steep street. Rocca di Papa is a marked object from every part of Rome. The houses are built up against the steep side of the Alban Mount, so that they can scarcely be distinguished from it, except by their whiteness. It swarms with wretched beggars now, as in the Middle Ages, I believe, it swarmed with feudal barons and their retainers. Beyond it we found ourselves upon the open hillside, with a great hollow plain to the left, where tradition says that Hannibal encamped when he would fain have taken Rome, but did not. I understood when I saw it how intensely irritating it must have been to have attained so much, and lost by so little. Looking from the mountains across to the misty city, it seems but one giant's stride, and it might have been reached. After the Campo di Annibale we ascended through woods again, but we were then so high that the leaves of the trees were not out. The ancient " Via Triumphalis" forms the last mile of the ascent. It is a very roughly-paved, narrow, little road—all those old Roman roads are marvellously narrow—and quite upsets modern ideas of dignity and a carriage-and-four. The Roman generals who were allowed an ovation used to ascend it on their march to the Temple of Jupiter, on the summit of the hill. Cæsar, when Dictator, enjoyed the honour.

It must have been a most picturesque and country-feeling march; not at all like what one imagines suited to a warlike triumphal procession. Monte Cavo must have been wooded then as now, for the sides are a great deal too steep for building; the Campagna, which we looked down upon, was doubtless more covered with buildings, but it could not have been what it was in the time of the Emperors; and though Cæsar may have traced the course of the Appian Way by some of the tombs which lined it on each side, he certainly could not have seen it in all its grandeur. I gained, in fact, quite a new idea of triumphal marches as we wended our way to the top of Monte Cavo; they seemed to become so much more simple and natural,—most especially when we reached the broad platform which forms the summit of the hill. Even if the view towards Rome and the north was in Cæsar's time architectural and human, yet Nemi and Albano must still have spread their calm lakes below; whilst, to the south, the scene could never have been anything but wild and solitary; hill stretching beyond hill, wood beyond wood, with the sparkling line of the Mediterranean their limit towards the west. One can imagine a man—weary with ambition— almost overwhelmed with the sense of intense repose when at the end of the long march he stood upon the summit of the mountain, and looked down upon that enchanting but most quiet view. A great Temple to Jupiter stood on the top of Monte Cavo in those days. It was 240 feet long, and 120 broad; and there were columns of white marble and giallo-antico, statues, and bas-reliefs, ornamenting it. The remains were to be seen late in the last century, but they are all gone now, except a few stones in a garden wall. The Passionists erected a convent on the site of the Temple; and Cardinal York, the last of the Stuarts, thought it necessary to destroy the ruins of the temple for the purpose of building a church.

There is a little room attached to the convent on the outside, where lady-visitors are allowed to dine if they like it; but M—— and I preferred a grey stone and the open air, and there we rested, and looked around and below us, only once disturbed by a portly-looking " brother," who was taking his solaitry walk round the convent walls. We made a quick descent to Frascati, passing again through Rocca di Papa, and then turning into a high road, along which we ambled on our donkeys for several miles, till about twelve o'clock we reached Frascati, and found the remainder of the party waiting for us at the hotel.

Dinner and rest were very pleasant then, and the afternoon was devoted to the Villas and Tusculum. Frascati is, as no doubt you know, a summer retreat for the Roman world. It is a good-sized town, with fascinating villas dotted about on the hills all round it; not the little square houses, with tiny gardens, which we call villas in England, but real Roman villas,—large houses, looking fast asleep with their closed blinds. In front, broad terraces and stone balustrades, statues and fountains; at the side, ilex and chestnut woods; behind, high hills, woody and rocky; below, the Campagna, and the mountains of the Abruzzi, the snow-covered Leonessa, the "lone Soracte," the far-off Siminian hills, and the gleaming Mediterranean—all familiar, yet all new, because regarded from a fresh point of view, and seen by a different light, and through a different atmosphere. For thus it is that Rome and its surroundings change like the sea, and vary their beauty every hour.

Cicero's Villa and Tusculum are high on the hills behind the villas,—so high, that, accustomed as I am becoming to the strange sites of ancient towns, I cannot help wondering how the people managed to live there comfortably. As for Cicero, once established in his villa, I should think he never left it. Tusculum must have been a citadel originally, and the town must have gathered at its base. What is now shown as the site of the city, seemed to me to admit of scarcely a foot of level ground, except perhaps about the spot on which the remains of the Theatre are still to be seen, and which was evidently excavated for the purpose. The seats of this Theatre are quite perfect. One can make out precisely where the musicians sat, and the play was acted. We sat down there, and L—— read out Macaulay's Lay of the Battle of Lake Regillus. The site of the Lake was below us to the right. It is now a dried-up circular depression, it was once a pool, about a quarter of a mile in circumference; but the size is in accordance with everything one sees connected with early Roman history.

The exceedingly small space within which so many note-worthy events occurred is indeed a continual surprise. The Sabines, the Volscians, the Latins, were comparatively within a stone's throw of Rome. But strength seems to lie in concentrated, not widespread energy; so it was with Greece, so I suppose one may say with truth it has been and now is in England itself; and this thought might stop the pride in enormous territory which all nations are, more or less, tempted to entertain.

We were shown a rough stone arch, dating from before the foundation of Rome, which was the entrance to a reservoir of water used for the citadel. It was in the steep side of the hill, and all round it was nearly equally steep. Where space could have been found for roads or buildings was more than I could understand.

I will not tire you with reckoning, much less describing, how many villas we saw that afternoon —all were beautiful, and each had some distinctive charm; but the view from the Mondragone Villa, belonging to Prince Borghese, struck me the most. The drive home was delicious; and after being on the back of a donkey for so many hours the carriage was most refreshing. We reached Rome about nine o'clock.

Yours, &c. &c.

P.S.—We have now and then amusing indications of political feeling. My donkey-man at Albano heard one of our party exclaim, " *Viva Garibaldi!* " "Ah!" he said aloud, " Garibaldi, Victor Emmanuel, or the Pope, it is all the same to me. I am a poor man, and have a son to take care of. I don't trouble myself about it." Then sidling up to me, he added, "We don't say '*Viva Garibaldi*' up at Albano, or the priests would put us in prison."

CHAPTER XIX.

ONE endeavour which I made in Rome was to discover why it was so resting and satisfying, as well as exciting, and it struck me at last that it was because of the completeness with which it enables a person to carry out the different trains of ideas which it awakens. Thought in Rome flows, as it were, in circles, crossing each other, yet distinct. There are no sudden interruptions, no breaks or jars. In other places an idea is suggested by some object, but either its beginning or its end is to be found elsewhere, and so the mind is sent off in a new direction, and in the very effort after continuity the chain is broken. To state this more plainly. In driving through the streets of Rome some object of antiquity meets the eye. There is no need to travel away from Rome in order to carry on the train of thought suggested by it; one may go back to Etruscan remains, and the mythical Roman kings, and so come down to the Republic and the Emperors, the transition period of barbarism, and the contests of the Middle Ages, and find specimens of each age close at hand;—the series is complete.

And it is the same with whatever subject is taken

up. Christianity, beginning with the early martyrs, and carried on through the growth of the Church and the rise of the Papacy;—sculpture in every form and every stage, pagan and Christian, Greek and mediæval;—painting, from its rise to its degeneracy;—and again, modern sculpture and modern painting,—these may be studied, not only thoroughly but easily. One lives, as it were, in a well-arranged library, and can find quotations for every topic brought under discussion.

After having once seen Rome thoroughly, so as to gain a complete, though necessarily superficial, idea of it as a whole, I can imagine a person sitting down quietly to study the distinct subjects which it brings before the mind with a fulness of satisfaction which could not possibly be met with elsewhere. In other cities you learn; in Rome you are taught. Almost without consciousness knowledge is acquired; and thus a week in Rome may be valued as a year spent away from it. This sense of the variety of Rome presses upon the mind painfully when one is endeavouring to gather up the impressions that have been received, and put them into some definite tangible form. Each drive through the streets has given one so much to dwell upon, that in despair one is tempted to put aside all effort after distinct thought, and merely to say of Rome, as every person must do, that it is a wonderful place.

The fountains alone would afford materials for a book. Some cities have one or two fountains striking for their quaintness or beauty; some—witness London—have one or two striking from their ugliness; but Rome is made up of fountains. They meet you in every direction, and in every form. The light-springing jets of St. Peter's, the torrent of the Fontana Paolina on the Janiculum, the confused rush of the waters of Trevi, or the full basin, from out of which rise the splendid bronze horses in front of the Quirinal, are but specimens of the abundance and freeness with which water has, from apparently very early times, been brought into Rome. And each fountain is a study, having some peculiarity, either of workmanship or position, to fix it in the memory. One learns to know Rome almost more by its fountains than its streets or churches; the magnificent view from the Janiculum, for instance, is impressed on the memory more by the rush of the Fontana Paolina, than by the Church of S. Pietro in Montorio, which is generally considered the important object marking the situation. And if, retracing the history of this lavish supply of water, the mind travels back, there is the Aqua Felice of that renovator yet destroyer of Rome, Sixtus the Fifth, still carrying on its daily work of bringing water into the city from the neighbourhood of Palestrina; whilst, crossing it, the tall arches of the Claudian

Aqueduct stalk proudly over the Campagna, for a while unbroken, then lost, then seen again as lichen-covered ruins, then as solitary bits of crumbling wall, scarcely to be distinguished in the distance.

Such beautiful framework for such lovely pictures do those arches form! I rode close up to them one day, and then passed slowly along, looking at the mountains as they were seen through them. Any one might have been a study for an artist. They, and the tomb of Cecilia Metella, and the Dome of St. Peter's, are the landmarks by which one is able to measure distance when riding across the Campagna. And they are always grand objects: nothing indeed is petty about Rome. A beautiful harmony exists between the city and its surrounding scenery. You are not called upon to throw yourself into a new state of feeling when you pass beyond the gates and enter upon the Campagna. As you ride or drive across it, and linger to mark the sunshine touching the ruin of some mediæval tower, some old tomb, or bit of broken wall, you are only carrying on the same thoughts which were awakened as you drove by the ruins of the Forum, or the Arch of Drusus; whilst the long purple shadows, and lakes of light, the flock of sheep following the shepherd, the solitary rider, the gentle-eyed, light-coloured oxen, grazing on the green banks, are as much in harmony with the majestic ruins of the Coliseum, as they are with the jagged yet soft mountains, tinted (as it has been said) like the hues on a dove's breast. Rome may touch many strings, but, as they vibrate, they form but one chord.

And so, in looking round to gather up the fragments of recollections that have been almost forgotten whilst dwelling upon prominent subjects, there is the less fear of bringing together incongruous elements, or forcing into connexion topics which are not naturally associated with one another. As the termination of our stay in Rome drew near, our days were given up to very heterogeneous sightseeing. The Lateran Museum, the Museum and Library of the Vatican, the Crypt of St. Peter's, the Barberini Library, were mixed up with researches after the localities of the Arch of Dolabella, and the Cloaca Maxima, and a drive on the Campagna to the Fountain of Egeria.

The Lateran Museum, like the gallery of Christian antiquities in the Vatican, is a mine of interest, if only a person knows how to dig into it. Both are the necessary completion of a visit to the Catacombs; but one cannot gain as much in the way of impressiveness from the former as from the latter.

Inscriptions and sarcophagi removed from their natural surroundings speak chiefly to the student; and the roughly-sculptured stone, which would have had a voice for every heart when lying in the empty grave-shelf of the Catacomb, is silent when placed as one amongst the many treasures collected in the Vatican or in the Lateran. No one indeed has a right to complain of this; the precious remains are no doubt far more carefully guarded now than they could have been if left where they originally were. I would only say that the *spirit* has in a very great degree departed from them, and a visit to the Christian gallery will probably be rather one of studious inquiry than of reverential feeling.

There are very beautiful specimens of heathen art also in the Lateran; and a comparison of these with the Christian remains was more interesting to me than the study of either alone.

In turning from one to the other, some vexation is at first excited on finding Christian art so manifestly inferior. The inscriptions are often rough and unfinished; and the strange figures on a Christian sarcophagus would, but for the subjects they represent, be a ludicrous contrast to the splendid bas-reliefs of the heathen monuments. It is only after a little thought that one can understand the truth which lies beneath this remarkable difference.

Early Christian art there is none; that is, if by early we mean in the time of the Apostles, and in the second century. The few inscriptions are rough and imperfect, for it was " to the poor the Gospel was preached;" and there is something far more touching in the half-formed, irregular letters which were the record of the immortal hope of the artisan, the mechanic, or, it might even be, the slave, than in the cold, careful, laborious record of heathen greatness. And when Christian art was able to exhibit itself more openly, heathen art was on the decline. That fact can be clearly traced. Though even then it would seem that the artistic element which remained was chiefly devoted to heathen purposes. We are apt to think that the world became Christian with Constantine—we forget what a long and fierce struggle must have taken place before the powers, which had for so many ages been devoted to the service of the pagan gods, could become the willing ministers to the glory of Christ; and whilst the conflict was yet being carried on, the barbarians had flooded the empire, and in that great deluge both Christian and heathen art alike for the time perished.

Next to the Christian antiquities, I suppose the Etruscan would be universally acknowledged as the most interesting; but the same remark may be made about the Etruscan Museum in the Vatican as about the Christian Museum in the Lateran. Each separate article has in it a mine of suggestion and information; but regarded as a whole, there is little to be said, except that the arts and civilization of the Etrurians were very astonishing. What, however, gives always matter for thought in such collections is the comparison between different ages and different states of society. There are in the Etruscan Museum some recumbent statues, taken from sarcophagi, with the heads curiously twisted sideways, which are not at all unlike the monumental figures, struggling after an upright position, that we sometimes see in an English Cathedral, dating, I think, about the reign of Elizabeth. Art seems to be at nearly the same stage in each; and I question whether, if the utensils and ornaments of the same English period were put side by side with the Etruscan, they would be found superior. Yet that there is a superiority, an immeasurable superiority, on the side of England every one believes;—only, from whence does it arise? That might lead one into an inquiry much too long and difficult to be entered upon; but it is surely good for us, in these days of nineteenth-century progress, to have brought before us vividly the fact, that neither science nor art can be the real standard by which to measure a nation's advance, since they may exist in almost the same degree in two periods; one of which is lost in the mists of what we consider a barbarous antiquity, whilst in the other is to be found the germ of all modern greatness.

The way in which history may be completely studied at Rome is nowhere better exemplified than in the Vatican and its museums, and St. Peter's considered together. St. Peter's alone is a complete volume, the contents of which are to be found not only in the Church, but the Crypt, with its tombs of the Popes, and its monuments and statues taken from the old Basilica; whilst the Rome of the present day may be read, as it were, from the balcony, at the base of the Ball: the view comprehending the whole of the city, and the Campagna from the Apennines to the Mediterranean. It is a view precisely suited to the building—grand and satisfying as a whole, though, like it, the details may be disappointing.

For this is the effect of St. Peter's as it is of Rome itself. The marble monuments, which are so splendid when contributing to the general impression, are very open to criticism when seen more nearly; they partake, in fact, of the spirit of the building, and are wanting in simplicity and devotional expression. Canova's monument to the Stuarts, which has been so much spoken of, is no exception. The names of James the Third, Charles the Third, and Henry the Ninth, arrest the attention and touch the heart of an English person; but apart from association, no one, I think, would be likely to linger in admiration over it. The bodies of the last three chiefs of the Stuart line rest in the Crypt. It is singular indeed to remark how St. Peter's gathers, in some form or other, its tribute of royalty from different countries. Monuments to Otho the Second and Christina of Sweden are to be found in the Crypt; whilst on the side of the wall, as you ascend the spiral staircase to the Dome, are inserted the names of the kings, queens, and princes, who in later days have completed their Roman pilgrimage by mounting to the Cupola or the Ball. Of course we looked for the name of our own prince, and boasted that he had been higher than any one else.

The Mosaics of St. Peter's, like the monuments, do not bear a close inspection. Placed, as they are, at an enormous height, delicacy of execution would be a loss. Yet they are wonderful for that very reason. It is not, however, till one has seen the studio in the Vatican, in which they are manufactured, that one can appreciate the skill which can so place the irregular pieces of different shades, side by side, as to form at a distance an exquisitely finished picture. The chief Mosaic work now going on is that for the Church of S. Paolo, which is to have a series of heads of the Popes above the arches in the nave as well as round the transept. The great advantage of Mosaics, besides their brilliant display of colour, is the way in which they can bear gold as an adjunct. No paintings could, for that reason, have the same effect.

The brilliancy and cheerfulness of St. Peter's and the Vatican are indeed quite startling to a person accustomed to the solemnity of gothic architecture and its customary decorations. The Vatican Library especially is a most remarkable contrast to the long, low-roofed college libraries of England, with their oak-carving and dusky volumes. It would make a most beautiful ball-room; and this, though not a very reverent idea, is really the first which suggests itself on entering. It is the very perfection of gay colouring,—full of arabesque ornaments, frescoes, and gilding; with splendid vases of malachite, oriental alabaster, and Sèvres china, the gifts of Emperors and Princes; and—not a book to be seen. There are closed cabinets against the wall, and attached to the pilasters; but what they contain you are only allowed to guess by seeing two or three opened by the *custode*, who allows you to glance for a moment at the stiff characters of Petrarch, and the clear, manly, and free writing of Tasso. You pass through the long rooms as you would through a suite of apartments in a palace, and leave it with much the same impression.

The Barberini Library, on the contrary, is really a library—a place for study, as quiet and solemnizing as the old rooms at Oxford; and the Abbé who had the care of it when we were there, and who was a perfect specimen of an old-fashioned Italian gentleman, showed his treasures with all the personal pride of a collector. He had most valuable manuscripts under his guardianship, but he scarcely seemed to recognize the duty of making them public, though he has lately printed some original letters of Galileo. The one thing I was inclined to covet myself was a missal, painted by one of Raphael's pupils, which was most beautiful; and there were some interesting original designs of an architect of the fifteenth century, containing sketches of Roman buildings as they were in his day;—the Porta Maggiore, for instance, with the Claudian Aqueduct carried over it. It made one feel what a complete blank the Rome of the Middle Ages is,—how its appearance is lost to us, whilst its life is only to be found in that of other nations. I think it is Dean Milman who remarks upon the power which Rome exercised on the further side of the Alps, whilst she was almost destroyed by the fierce dissensions of her own children on the near side. Mediæval Rome is merely the crumbling dust which buries the past, and is a foundation for the superstructure of the present.

CHAPTER XX.

46, *Via Sistina*, *May* 4*th*, 1861.

My dear ——,

We have just returned from our last Roman expedition—alas! We were to have been absent two nights, and to have seen Subiaco, which is up amongst the mountains; but there was a difficulty about the carriage-road,—in fact, there is none to Subiaco itself, so we were obliged to give up the intention, and content ourselves with Palestrina (the ancient Præneste,) and Tivoli instead. We went—a party of seven, besides a servant, and carried all kinds of appurtenances with us, for Palestrina is a most wretched place. It lies at the foot of the Sabine range, quite at the extremity, and is spoken of as a town, and has centuries of historical associations and relics attached to it:—Pelasgic architectural remains,—villas and temples of the Roman Republic,—and walls and gateways of the Middle Ages; but it is the dirtiest, most poverty-stricken, most entirely wretched and hopeless place I ever visited. I wish you could have seen us after our drive across the Campagna, and our ascent of a very steep hill—bordered by a wall of those wonderful Pelasgic stones, which make one think of the days of the giants—stopping in a narrow street, at the entrance of a still narrower alley, and watching for the return of the adventurous members of our party, who had volunteered to examine the capabilities of what was called the Inn. After all there was not much use in inquiring, for whether good or bad, we had nothing else to choose from; and when we were told that it would *do*, we knew that the words only meant—it must do. And it was a *must*—a very dire necessity. Such an entrance—so unutterably dirty!—one could only pass on and try to forget it. Happily we had our man-servant and provisions; and though the rooms were miserable, with most scanty furniture, brick floors, and very cold, we thought we had enough of interest in store to make us overlook discomfort.

But Palestrina was unquestionably a disappointment. Excavations have been going on lately, and we were told that they were much more important than those at Ostia; but when we came to inquire, we found that they had recently been covered up, and everything valuable carried away to Rome. So we had nothing to do but to make the best of nature's antiquities, and mount the hill to the Citadel; stopping on our way to see the remains of Sylla's Temple of Fortune, and a wonderful specimen of mosaic pavement, evidently

Egyptian in design, and a never-failing topic of discussion for antiquaries. Again my mind was perplexed as to how the world in those days ever reached their temples and houses. They were built more like eagles' nests on the sides of rocks than like human habitations. Probably, however, my own sense of difficulty and insecurity was enhanced by the fact, that I ascended to the citadel of Palestrina seated on the back of a donkey, and on a saddle which had no pommel, or protection of any kind, except a slight elevation in front, to which I clung in the best way I could, whilst the animal scrambled up a path of steps and rolling stones, in some parts seemingly as steep as the gable of a house. I could have reached the citadel in no other way, for it is built on a height of more than two thousand five hundred feet above the sea. We found some miserable hovels, and more miserable inhabitants, on the summit; the children—little atoms of humanity—crawled out of the dark doorways to beg for *baiocchi*. They seemed out of the way of all prospect of education or employment. If it had not been for the little church built in the midst, I should have been entirely heart-sick in looking at them. But the Roman Catholics give us a lesson in this respect; they leave no place, however poor, without some provision for worship. There is a picturesque ruin of a mediæval castle on the very summit of the citadel hill, and a splendid view all round—a new view—commanding the Volscian mountains, but it has not the softness of the views from Albano. Palestrina altogether is a stern and earthly place. Hannibal reconnoitred Rome from it, so it is said, and such a warlike association suits it well. Whatever the town may have been in former days, it could never, I should think, be in any way restored now, it is so inaccessible. We found a quantity of terra-cotta vases and votive offerings taken from the excavations, and lying on the floor in a loft; but there was nothing for which it would have been worth our while to come so far, and bear the inconveniences of such a wretched inn.

Tivoli, the next day, was very different. We had a long and lovely drive; starting soon after eight, and reaching the lane which turns off to Hadrian's Villa before twelve. The road is carried through a wooded ravine nearly the whole way. I mention Hadrian's Villa, because we had engaged to meet a party from Rome there, and we were so happily punctual, that we joined them precisely as they arrived.

The remains of the baths, porticoes, halls, library, which are included in the Villa, cover an immense extent of ground; cypresses, pines, and shrubs are intermixed, and the whole is excessively picturesque, but, as some one suggested, not half so imposing as many lesser ruins, because, after all, the Villa was but a *made up* place, with more show than solidity. Don't think that was an observation of mine. I have not lived long enough in Rome to despise the age of the Emperors; but they and their works are evidently not recognised as *antiques* by persons who are thoroughly Roman in spirit. Tivoli is not above a mile from Hadrian's Villa. It is an ascent all the way; chiefly through a grove of olives, very old—the twisted trunks and grey foliage most singular to an English eye. We drove to the Villa d'Este, and had luncheon on a covered terrace overlooking the gardens; and then mounted donkeys and made the regular sight-seeing "*giro.*" I despair of descriptions,—but Tivoli is wholly unlike any view of it which I ever saw. You generally see represented a small cascade falling down a gloomy ravine, with a little temple at the top; whereas the cascade is but one very small portion of the real Tivoli. This, as a whole, consists of a winding, deep, and steep ravine, with the Anio flowing through it; on one side the town—built close to the edge of the precipice, and on the other, a beautiful wood of olives, from which you look across to the red cliffs, the woods and gardens of the villas, and the little cascades, or *cascatelle.*

The great fall has changed in position since Gregory the Sixteenth diverted the course of the Anio, spoilt the original waterfall, and saved the town from being destroyed by the undermining of the water. It was formerly close to the town and the temple; now the river flows at some little distance, and rushing through two tunnels cut in the rock, falls into the ravine from a height of more than 300 feet.

Tivoli is a complete tourist's place, and one can but take the tourist's ride or walk; but every step of the way is lovely, especially when one escapes the little well-kept walks which wind down the cliff by the side of the old waterfall. The Temple of Vesta is like that in Rome, very small, and too closely encircled by other buildings to be viewed to advantage. Of course Tivoli has the accessories of mountains and the Campagna, seen from every height, and especially to be admired from the Villa d'Este, which has a foreground of pines and olives, a long cypress avenue, flights of steps, and fountains. There is a resemblance to Frascati in it; but though in some respects more beautiful, it is not so free. We were at Rome by eight o'clock, not sorry to have the prospect of home comforts after our experience of a Palestrina Inn. Tivoli has deepened my conviction of the charms of Rome, for it is so within reach, that one may consider it as belonging to the city, as much as Richmond belongs to London. Yours, &c., &c.

Via Sistina, May, 1861.

MY DEAR ——,

You will have rather a discursive letter, for we are in the midst of the bustle of departing preparations,—fragments of sight-seeing, good-byes, and packings, mingled with discussions upon the respective merits or demerits of crowded steamers, with no place but the deck to sleep on, and country inns, which, as likely as not, may be the centre of attraction, not only to ourselves, but to robbers. I don't mean that we may probably be robbed at the inns, but that robberies are not unknown soon after travellers have started from them. However, we are going to try the land journey, for no cabin can be secured from Naples; and as the individuals who last committed a robbery have been taken, and several persons have gone quite safely since by Siena, which is our route, we trust it may be our fate to arrive safely at our journey's end. I can't help being amused at the calm way in which we talk over the probabilities of being robbed,—it has become rather a pleasant excitement than not. Some friends of ours went through the ordeal in 1848, and have given us full instructions what we are to do;—how we are to "come when we are called, and do as we are bid," and not look alarmed when a man stands a couple of yards from us with a musket pointed at us. What the brigands most dislike is being kept waiting, so we are going to put up a little money in readiness for them. I heard M—— ask just now, when inquiring about some financial arrangements, whether the money for the robbers had been remembered. Seriously, we do not think there is any reason to be afraid, only we are just so cautious, that we mean to send everything we care for by sea.

We have been gathering up the ends of business and mixing pleasure with them, in the form of visits to Castellani's and Saulini's. Castellani is the great Roman jeweller. He made the sword which was presented to the Emperor, and, as a natural consequence, he is now an exile, and his business is carried on by his brother, who not improbably will be an exile too before long. It is grievous to see how all persons of talent and influence are by degrees leaving this unhappy city. Doctor Pantaleoni, the first physician in Rome, was sent off the other day; his wife, so I was told, was not permitted to follow him till she had promised not to return; and the Government were so petty in their tyranny, that when at length she did go, they would not give a permission to some gentleman who was her friend to accompany her to Civita Vecchia, simply because she was the Signora Pantaleoni. This is by way of parenthesis; it has nothing to do with the display of jewels, except that Signor Castellani so evidently felt we were *sympathisers,* and took pleasure in our visit as he would in that of personal friends. His gold ornaments are the most fashionable things now—they are almost all copies of the Etruscan. As copies, they are perfect; but it is a question in my own mind, though I know it is a heresy, whether, in themselves, they are so remarkably beautiful; whether, in fact, the admiration lavished upon them is not bestowed more upon the association and the delicate workmanship than the design. It is this which has struck me in all the modern works of art or ornament which I have seen since I have been in Rome. Saulini's cameos are exquisite, but they are all reproductions; and it is the same with the Mosaics. You may go to twenty shops, and you will see precisely the same views and ornaments in each. And if, with all the boast of progress in the nineteenth century, we cannot surpass in beauty of design the unknown people who inhabited Italy before Rome was founded, I really do not see what we have to pride ourselves upon. Early Christian imitations dispute the palm with the Etruscan. They, of course, have a different value, but I don't think it is pleasant to see them made fashionable. If they are worn with a Christian feeling, it is all well; but the Dove and the olive branch, and the Lamb resting upon the Book with seven seals, are designs scarcely appropriate for a ball-dress ornament.

Amongst other bits of sight-seeing we have made pilgrimages to the Tarpeian rock, (which of course you know forms part of the Capitoline hill,) and to the Medici Gardens (*vide* "Transformation" for the first, and "Mademoiselle Mori" for the second). The Tarpeian rock, I had always been told, was a mistake in the present day, whatever it may have been in former times, so I was not disappointed when I saw it. There is, first of all, a doubt about the site; so you are obliged to suspend and divide your classical enthusiasm, unless you can do as we did,—look at one, and think of "Transformation," and at the other, and recal the death of an ancient Roman. Anyhow, a fall from either part of the rock would be very awkward, and must, in all probability, be fatal. The first site, a little court surrounded by a low wall, is exactly described in "Transformation;" and when you look over the wall you gaze down into another square court below, with buildings all round it, very unlike the base of the ancient Roman Citadel, but not therefore the less likely to be the scene of a modern murder. The real site of the Tarpeian rock, I suspect, must have been on the other side of the Capitoline, looking towards the Forum. It is reached after mounting a long flight of steps, walking half-way down a street, and then turning into a little garden, the perfection of Italian rural simplicity;—flowers in profusion, trickling water, narrow paths, and low-border hedges, all very luxuriant and very untidy. Old Rome,—the Forum, the Coliseum, the Triumphal Arches,—and a confused medley of cottages and gardens, lie below, with the Alban Mount in the distance; and I confess that, if I had to live in Rome, and could choose my residence only for the sake of its associations, the neighbourhood of the Tarpeian rock is just the spot I should fix upon. As for the rock itself, you look over a wall into a court, as you do from the other side; but there is more of the precipice visible, and one can better understand from that position what the height of the Capitol originally was, and how it could have been built upon and defended.

The Medici gardens are nothing very surprising; they are on the summit of the Pincian, and there are the usual long walks, and yew hedges, and statues, with charming views. The description of the "Bosco" in "Mademoiselle Mori" is exact, as indeed all the descriptions in the book are, so far as I could learn. We have paid a parting visit to a Villa,—the Wolconsky,—Russian or Polish of course. It is a complete bit of Rome, modern and ancient combined;—acacias, ivy, and roses twining together and forming a long avenue, and the Claudian Aqueduct being part of the garden wall. It will be my last reminiscence of Rome, and a most lovely one. We hope to go on Thursday, or rather we do not hope it, for we would give a great deal to stay, most especially as it is Ascension Day, and we are forced into being heathens against our will. The question of necessity is one with which of course I need not trouble you; but we really have no choice. I grieve, amongst other things, at the scandal we give to Josephine, who is a very sincere but liberal-minded Romanist; and is quite surprised, and I think rather pleased, to find that we do not ignore times and seasons, and can recognise the duty of attendance at church-services oftener than one day in seven. She does not at all understand our travelling on Ascension Day, and all we can say is, that we would not do it if we could avoid it.*

Yours, &c. &c.

---

* The pleasure which will ever stand out prominently in the retrospect of my last days at Rome is a visit—the second I had made—to Mrs. Barrett Browning. The short intercourse has now been rendered so sacred by death, that I only refer to it from the wish to express, not merely the admiration which all must feel for her great poetical powers, but the personal regard inspired by the charm of her winning manner, her cordiality and quick sympathy, her self-restraint and thoughtful consideration, when, in the course of conversation, any sentiments at variance with her own were brought forward. Mrs. Barrett Browning was the one person in Rome of whom every one who knew her spoke with respectful affection; and, slight as was our acquaintance, it has left an ineffaceable impression of the working of that spirit of Charity which, when all shades and differences of opinion shall be lost in the light of God's knowledge, will, we are told, last for ever.

CHAPTER XXI.

Siena, May 13*th,* 1861.

My dear ——,

We are so far on our way to Florence—our journey not having been wholly unadventurous. We left Rome on Thursday. I was hopeful almost to the last that something might occur to detain us, but all our plans, unhappily, went smoothly, and there was no excuse for delay; so we met the rest of our party at the Porta del Popolo, at seven o'clock in the morning, and drove past the English Church instead of entering it. We had a journey of fifty miles that day to Viterbo,—over the Campagna for a long distance, and then ascending the hills, from which there were lovely views as we looked back upon Rome. The foregrounds were always wooded, and we passed the quiet Lake of Bolsena, famous, alas! for malaria. Soracte, to the north-east, gained in grandeur what it lost in softness; and the rugged hills, and ravines, and woods, which stretched away in that direction, gave one some idea of what would have been the beauty of the scenery if we had taken the road to Florence through Perugia, which would have led us amongst them. *Voiturier* travelling is very slow, but I like it extremely, it is so domestic. We were a large party, in three carriages; so we felt quite bold when we thought of the robbers. The first day was supposed to be the dangerous day, and we congratulated ourselves accordingly, when, late in the evening, we rattled through the narrow, paved streets of Viterbo, (paved all over they were,) and found ourselves safe. We had fair accommodation at the hotel, and our arrival was quite an excitement, we were so many in number. Viterbo is not much accustomed, I should think, to any excitement, except of a political kind. Illuminations were going on for a Bishop, newly appointed; but the waiter ventured to communicate to us the fact that he would willingly have had one for Victor Emmanuel. We started the next morning all together, but parted company in the middle of the day; two carriages turning off to Orvieto, and the other, containing our own special party, going on to Radicofani. We stopped in the middle of the day at Aquapendente, which I have marked in my journal as "dirty, dull, and dolorous." The two last epithets may be applied to a considerable portion of our road, especially as we drew near to Radicofani, and began to ascend the mountain—and not a tree nor a house was to be seen. Radicofani, which is in the Tuscan territory, is an old hunting-seat of the Grand Dukes, now converted into an hotel; round it are gathered a few wretched cottages, and the ruins of the castle of a robber-chief are to be seen on the square summit of the mountain just above it; the hill being in shape very like a large cake, and a remarkable object for miles round.

The inn was a huge, rambling house, with long corridors, and large half-furnished rooms with immense fireplaces. We piled up logs of wood, and made ourselves very comfortable; but it was just the kind of house in which one might have been nervous to any extent. I had a room which had once been occupied by Pius the Seventh, so said a tablet over the door. It was very large, and looked out upon a tidy garden, having a bleak expanse of mountains all round. A nightingale sang to me cheerily, but everything else was as dreary as could be externally.

The first thing we heard the next morning was that, four hours after we had passed, the *diligence* from Florence to Rome had been stopped and robbed at some little distance from Radicofani, by eight men. Will you be shocked, if I confess that I was rather pleasantly excited at the news? It made me feel that I had not been frightened for nothing; and my sympathies were the less called forth as, I believe, the passengers were all men, and no one seemed to have suffered particularly, or lost much, though doubtless it was very unpleasant at the time. Moreover, when we stopped at Buonconvento in the middle of the day, we were told that the robbers had all been taken, and had just been brought into the town. They were said to be galley-slaves, whom the Pope had just set free. Of course there was some commotion in the place in consequence, but all of a quiet kind. Buonconvento is in the new Italian dominions, and there was freedom of thought and speech in consequence. The Cameriera looked out of the window, and said to me, in a pitying tone, that the people in the Roman States were discontented; and when we went to dinner we found she had placed a little bust of Victor Emmanuel, as an ornament, on the table. It was strange to ourselves the feeling we had of being able to say and do what we liked the moment we were out of the Papal States. We drove out of the town actually followed by the robbers, who, placed in carts and guarded by police, were, like ourselves, on their way to Siena, though their unhappy destination was the prison.

The change in the appearance of the country had been quite remarkable, from the moment we entered the Tuscan territory. Even before we reached Buonconvento, we noticed that the cottages and little villages were neater, and that the country was better cultivated; and as we drew nearer to Siena, this was still more evident. Siena itself is a very striking place. It stands high amongst rather barren hills—which, however, are under cultivation. The entrance by the road to Rome is through a long avenue and gateway; the streets are very narrow, the houses very tall; the object of all building seems to be to keep out the sun. There is a great deal of interest in it, but— it is not Rome. I begin to feel that painfully. If I had seen Siena before Rome, I should have been delighted with it. It is pleasant, however, to be in a town which is not degraded and oppressed, and where the people have a thriving, contented air. If I were but learned in art, I could write you a volume upon the peculiarities of the Cathedral, and the Sienese artists. The latter form a school by themselves, and I am learning to distinguish them by the remarkable length of the nose in all the pictures of the Madonna. The Sienese school was a very early one—the earliest of all in Italy indeed, so it is said. There is a charming collection of its pictures in the Istituto delle Belle Arti. Painters, of whom one never heard before, become quite familiar after seeing it. Then there are other, scattered about in churches. One might spend weeks in seeing and studying them all. A picture of the "Ecce Homo," by Sodoma, which is praised so much in "Transformation," I was disappointed in; but there are others wonderfully beautiful,—a Monica and Augustine in the Church of S. Agostino especially. The picture itself is described as "Christ at the Cross, surrounded by Saints;" Augustine is kneeling, and looking up to our Lord, and Monica looks down upon her son. A most perfect portraiture of feeling it is;—years of life's history—thought, and suffering, and thankfulness—condensed into the expression of the moment. I have become learned also in the history of St. Catharine, and have visited what was her house, or rather her father's. The old kitchen has been converted into an oratory, and the fireplace is still to be seen under the altar; but the attempt to consecrate all these places utterly destroys any feeling they might otherwise inspire. If people would but learn that truth and simplicity are God's consecration, and that nothing more is needed to touch the heart, it would be a great comfort to all persons who are not blessed with a superabundant amount of credulity.

St. Catharine is depicted in every church one enters. If a fresco of Sodoma's, in the Church of S. Domenico, might be accepted as a likeness—which of course it may not—she must have been extremely lovely; but the legends connected with her are, to me, very painful, and I turn from the most beautiful paintings representing them with a sense of repulsion. They are very like those connected with St. Francis, and a picture of an ecstasy chills me into complete unfeelingness; but, then, I am not an Italian.

One learns at Siena what frescoes may be when well preserved. There are some magnificent Pintrosicchios in the library attached to the Cathedral, as fresh, apparently, as when they were first painted. Frescoes generally are tantalising; witness Michael Angelo's in the Sistine Chapel, which, as they fade year by year, become necessarily to the ordinary eye a mass of faint colour without definite form. The Cathedral is a building to wonder at and delight in; incorrect, I believe, in architecture, but most brilliant in colour, and perfect in workmanship. After the ugly Roman churches, one gazes upon it with intense satisfaction—not the solemnising, reverential satisfaction which our own grey cathedrals inspire, for it is made up of red, and white, and black, and gold, and rich sculpture and delicate tracery, and looks as bright as an Italian sky, and is as gay in its effect as a Roman Catholic ceremony; but then it suits the place, the people, and the religion, and the longer we live the more we must all learn to appreciate the value and necessity of *suitableness*. I hope it is not irreverent to quote Scripture upon the subject, and say that the endeavour to " put new cloth into an old garment," or the reverse, is too often the blunder of life, only recognised as such when it is too late.

We have driven a little way out of the town, and gained a tolerable view of the country. There is always an object for a drive in Italy—some church or convent to be seen—and we went to the Osservanza, a Franciscan convent, where there were some beautiful specimens of Luca della Robbia's terracotta work. It must always, I should think, be an inferior kind of art, and one does not wonder that it has not been more followed up; but the expression thrown into the faces is wonderful. There was one subject in the Osservanza—"The Nativity," which, in that respect, was quite equal to any sculpture or painting I ever saw.

Our Orvieto party have rejoined us. They have had a real, instead of a possible experience of the adventurous kind, for they fell in with an earthquake, which has been visiting both Orvieto and Chiusi. They found the terrified people sitting outside their houses, expecting what, they were told by the priests, was the judgment of Heaven upon them for their rebellion against the Pope. They felt a shock themselves at Chiusi, where they slept; and say of it, as every one else says of an earthquake, that it is an untold horror.

I don't feel that I have done Siena justice, especially as to its scenery. It is towards Radicofani that it is so bleak, otherwise the country is more than pretty, being broken up into ravines, with a sufficient quantity of wood and cultivation to be home-like; and standing so high as the town does, the views all round are extensive. Moreover, it has the advantage of a healthy summer climate, and altogether it deserves and bears a highly respectable character for agreeableness.

Yours, &c. &c.

CHAPTER XXII.

Villino della Torre, Florence, May 16th, 1861.

My dear ——,

You will be glad to know that we are safe at Florence, though there was no danger in the railway from Siena. Florence is fascinating, quite as much so as it has been described. The contrast with Rome is most singular. All here is bright, prosperous, and well-finished — no ruins, no dirt; the streets are regular and well-kept, the people happy and industrious, and the country lovely beyond description. I was at Bello Sguardo last night, and saw the sunset over the Carrara mountains—seventy miles off; the valley of the Arno being spread out below me, studded with villas and peasants' cottages, and rich in cultivation. On the other side the view extends thirty miles—over Florence to the mountains, amongst which lies Vallombrosa. The Duomo and the Campanile stand up grandly in the centre of the city, and beyond them rise three tiers of hills—the Arno winding at their base. And such adjuncts to the views there were last night! A quaint Italian villa, untrimmed, yet tasteful, as all such places are;—wholly without pretension, and only ornamented with flowers—orange-blossoms, heliotropes, verbenas, carnations, &c.—and paintings of the Madonna and the saints by the old Sienese masters. Cream, and wood-strawberries, and country bread, reminded me of the profuse hospitality of an English farm-house; and as we sat at tea the musical bells from the towers of Florence sounded for the Venti-quattro, as it is called—the summons for the evening prayer to the Virgin. We drove home in an open carriage, enjoying the delicious summer warmth, and I for one rejoicing in seeing fire-flies. The weather has been excessivly hot since we arrived, but I delight in it. We have a most luxurious *appartement*, with all the appurtenances of a home.

Yesterday, and the day before, I was occupied in seeing pictures at the Pitti Palace and the Uffizi. The former contains the gems. I really dread to mention pictures, so few people comparatively care to hear about them. If E—— is interested to know which I like best, tell her that there are two of Raphael's portraits of Maddalena and Angelo Doni—the latter especially, which would enchant her; also a magnificent Leo the Tenth. The Madonna della Seggiola is perfect in finish and in colouring, but I doubt whether, as a whole, it has the reverential and retiring expression which one would expect. Michael Angelo's picture of "The

Three Fates" satisfies me more than anything else I have seen of his. It is just the subject which suits him. A Fate would seem to be the nearest approach to his perception of a woman. There is one very famous picture of Andrea del Sarto's in the Pitti, which gives quite a new impression of his powers. It has a strength and dignity which most of his other pictures want. It is called "The Disputa;" the subject being a discussion upon the doctrine of the Trinity between some of the Apostles and saints. One might stand for an hour looking at it, and studying the different meanings of the countenances. Then there are some splendid pictures by Fra Bartolommeo, with whom I am just beginning to make acquaintance; a most beautiful Pietà—the face of the Virgin absolutely perfect in its sorrowful tenderness,—and a single figure of St. Mark. Also some Peruginos, beautiful in expression as all his are; and a Philip the Second, by Titian, which really makes one feel that Philip might once have been a person to inspire respect, if not love.

The Pitti is a comfortable place to go to,—not overpowering. The rooms are square, without interest in themselves; but there are seats, which I mention because I suffered so much in the Munich Gallery once for want of them. The palace on the exterior is a large, handsome, yet, upon the whole, ugly stone house, if you can understand what that means.

The actual material is handsome, but it is square and straight. There are no colonnades, or wings, or porticoes; but the eye takes in the whole at once. It stands in a kind of open Piazza, and has the extensive Boboli Gardens behind it; but its general effect is that of heaviness and dulness.

In the Uffizi, which is, strictly speaking, a collection of public offices, there are very long galleries and suites of small rooms, with one circular apartment, called the Tribune, in the centre, which contains all the best pictures. There every one congregates, for the very vastness of the collection makes one shrink from attempting it as a whole. The real pleasure would be to make it a place for study, beginning with the old masters in the first long gallery, whom one learns more and more to admire, and understand, and distinguish; the latter being a great element in admiration. Upon first beginning a picture-seeing course, all painters before Raphael are put down as belonging to the same date. The Venus de' Medici, and several other remarkable statues, are in the Tribune; but I must own that I gave all my time and attention to the paintings. Raphael's Madonna del Cardellino is one of the most noted; and it is very lovely, though it does not equal the Madonna del Gran Duca, which I forgot to mention as amongst the treasures of the Pitti Palace. The latter was so valued by the late Grand Duke, that he always kept it in his private apartments, and only left it at last because he departed in such haste that he had no time to pack it up. Of all Raphael's Madonnas, *that* is the one I admire the most. There is a Julius the Second, also by Raphael, which is magnificent; it is a duplicate of the picture in the Pitti. Raphael's portraits I always look upon without a thought of criticism; they are accepted at once as the face of the living being. Fra Bartolommeo appears again in the Tribune in two single pictures of Job and Isaiah, which in some respects resemble the St. Mark in the Pitti. He seems to have been distinguished for these grand figures; but that of Isaiah is, to me, wanting in age and dignity.

Then there is a charming Andrea del Sarto—a Holy Family—besides two Peruginos,—one a picture of St. Sebastian,—a subject in which the artists of that age appear to have delighted, and in which they seem always to have been most successful. The beauty of youth, and the dignity of suffering combined, naturally, I suppose, affect one readily. St. Sebastian and the "Annunciation" are, generally speaking, the two most satisfactorily-treated subjects which I have remarked. The "Annunciation" is always particularly beautiful. There is one by Orgagna in the long gallery, as you enter the Uffizi, the remembrance of which is a treasure for life. One must sometimes venture to differ from good authorities, so I will mention, as another painting very admirable, (by admirable meaning worthy to be admired,) a Correggio,—the "Repose in Egypt." I believe it is quite condemned by Kügler, but I really cannot help that. It was, to me, the most beautiful Correggio I had ever seen. Neither must I forget the "Meeting of the Virgin and Elizabeth," by Albertinelli, in a room near the Tribune,—a picture which struck me the very instant I entered. I knew nothing about the painter, who was really a friend of Fra Bartolommeo; but it was impossible to pass it by. There are but the two figures: the calm, aged Elizabeth, and the lovely Virgin; they stand out most strikingly, telling their story at a moment's glance. It is one of the pictures constantly photographed, so I am able to retain and acknowledge my admiration with a consciousness of being "all right."

One delightful room in the Uffizi contains portraits of all the great painters, chiefly by themselves. Raphael is beautiful, as he always is; and Leonardo da Vinci has certainly set off his fine face to the best advantage by his most exquisite finish. Quintin Matsys makes his own portrait a covering for that of his wife, which is painted inside the case, or frame, that holds his likeness. This fashion of placing one picture within another strikes one as strange. There is an Albert Dürer either in the Pitti or the Uffizi, I forget which, hidden by a picture of Brenghel's. I suppose it is a sign of reverence,—a wish to hide a great treasure from a careless eye; but it is rather provoking, as one might so easily miss what is well worth seeing. But I really must not go on any longer about pictures. A chief pleasure in writing down an opinion about them is that of imprinting it upon one's own memory; otherwise, when seeing such an immense number, it is difficult to carry away a distinct impression of any. The pictures in the Uffizi are allowed to be copied freely. In one long gallery you may see the artists ranged one behind another, each with his "gem" before him. To look at them is rather disenchanting. Before seeing the original, one can admire a copy "*con amore;*" but when the two are put side by side, one begins to see that after all there is something in the mind of the original artist which is seldom, if ever, caught by another, however great his skill in imitation.

Yours, &c. &c.

CHAPTER XXIII.

The great distinction between Florence and Rome seems to me to be that the former has, in comparison with the latter, no soul; which is a cant and somewhat sentimental mode of expression, but must be accepted as embodying a true meaning. The soul of a place is, of course, the aggregate of the deeds, and words, and thoughts of the men who have lived in it, or been connected with it. It is not only that a city which takes its rise from the Middle Ages cannot compete with one which dates from seven hundred years before the birth of Christ, but that all the associations and events connected with Florence are of a less ennobling character. Florence and the Medici are inseparable,—and what can be said of the Medici? what can be felt about them? how can they inspire enthusiasm? All connected with them is luxurious and selfish—great vice, with a thin veneer of art. And it is quite strange how one feels this in Florence. The spirit of the Medici haunts the city to this day; and there is nothing before them,—no

Palace of the Cæsars, no ruins of the Forum to carry the mind back to the wonders and speculations of antiquity,—and nothing since, if one excepts the stirring associations of the great Cinque-Cento Hall, in the Palazzo Vecchio, in which the Deputies met to vote the annexation of Tuscany to the kingdom of Sardinia.

Present history in Florence is, in fact, much more important and exciting than past. There is but one individual who in the midst of those too famous days of the Medici stands out with real elevation of character,—Savonarola; and it is a significant fact, that his life, written by Villeri, with a full appreciation of his character, has within the last year been published in Florence. This absence of nobility in the history of a city naturally affects a stranger much more than a resident. Florence must be a very pleasant place to live in. It has all the charm which art and refinement can give. Nothing can be more lovely than the Val d'Arno, studded with villas, and shut in by purple mountains; and for mere amusement, no one would wish for pleasanter public drives than the wooded Cascine, having the Arno on one side, and on the other the broad meadows, in which the cattle are feeding as in an English park. Then the town has a well-built, prosperous, substantial, and withal uncommercial look. Though there are no very grand

squares, or wide streets, yet the public buildings,
—the Palazzo Vecchio, the Palazzo Pitti, the Bargello, the Palazzo Ricardi, the Palazzo Strozzi, and
others,—are solemnly handsome, and concentrate in
themselves a great deal of historical interest. The
Loggia of Orgagna also, in front of the Uffizi, is
quite peculiar to Florence, and would alone give
a special character to the city. Nowhere else
would be seen a collection of splendid statues,
placed under beautiful arcades, and free to the
inspection of every passer-by. These things give
to Florence its unmistakeable air of refinement
and cultivated taste. Neither is it so large as to
oppress you with the feeling of being in a town.
Standing upon the Ponte Carraja, and then looking up and down the Arno, you can enjoy both
the city and the country. Behind you is the
small collection of streets and buildings gathered
round the Palazzo Pitti, and the Boboli gardens,
both of which lie on the south side of the river.
Before you, to the right, extends the busy part
of the town; and to the left your eye may pass
along the woods of the Cascine, and rest upon
the distant mountains. And nothing in all this
jars upon the sense of cheerful enjoyment. You
have no thought of mobs or poverty in Florence.
It is the city of the "upper ten thousand." Giotto's
most exquisite Campanile, with its inlaid coloured

marbles, and delicately worked carving, is the perfect embodiment of its spirit. But—is it severe to say?—it is all of the earth, earthly. Drive through the streets of Rome, and you return actually oppressed with the questions which have been suggested to your mind. You are not satisfied with anything, past, present, or future, but you must think;—you must settle, or endeavour to settle for yourself, what the world's history means. Drive through the streets of Florence, and you do not think or wonder; you simply accept earth and its enjoyments, and that in the most tempting and delusive form of calm, dignified, artistic beauty. If mankind, as they are, were to be immortal upon earth, Florence might be (so far as satisfaction was possible) a thoroughly satisfying resting-place.

For although thus earthly it is essentially different from Paris. There is nothing in the least frivolous about it; and it can scarcely be called gay—if by gaiety is meant brightness without depth. There is, indeed, some display of fashion in the Cascine, where carriages all meet in one central open space in front of the royal dairies; and where gentlemen loungers go from one to the other, talking to their acquaintances; yet this is but a small element in Florentine life—very little of it is seen in the streets. No doubt there has been a change since the Grand Duke's departure. Some friends of mine, living in Florence, told me they could perceive it, but Florence could never have been merely fashionable; and this to many persons must constitute a great attraction, since nothing is more wearisome than a fashionable social atmosphere, if you cannot throw yourself into it. What there is below this external prosperous surface, a stranger, spending only three weeks there, cannot be supposed to know. That it is essentially a *respectable* movement which has revolutionized Florence is evident, if it were only from the order and decorum of the streets. The public feeling there, as in Rome, seems strongest in the middle classes—amongst the professional men, the artists, and tradespeople; and no Government can long stand against a pressure from such a source. We were in the Pitti Palace one morning, and heard the conversation of three artists who were discussing the question of the National Fête, —forbidden by the Archbishop and the Priests, but which the people were resolved to celebrate by singing a *Te Deum* in the Piazza della Indipendenza. One of them said, that "he had been trying to persuade several people not to be afraid to join the meeting, for it was quite clear that Heaven was not displeased with them; if it had been otherwise, they would by this time have found themselves again under the chains of the Austrians." Now this was a chance speech, but I suppose it may be taken as a sample of the tone which pervades the people generally,—not rebellious, not irreligious, but considerate and resolved. If the Florentines are ever driven into excesses, it will surely be by the errors of their rulers, and not by their own wilfulness.

CHAPTER XXIV.

Villino della Torre, May, 1861.

My dear ——,

.... Florence is wholly unlike Rome. It is difficult to carry on connected ideas *here*. I go to numberless places, and see numberless interesting things; but one can't condense and group them as one does at Rome. The Villas are enchanting. Lord Normanby's, for instance, and the Villa Capponi, which adjoins it, are more beautiful in themselves— taking in the near view of the Val d'Arno and the hills, which adds such a charm to them—than any private villas at Rome, even including the Pamphila Doria; and they have this additional advantage, that you feel you could live in them all the year round. But (of course there is a " but"—a " roc's egg"—to everything in this world) there is nothing to make up for the freedom of the Campagna. In the immediate neighbourhood of Florence your mind travels along dusty roads between walls and vineyards and gardens, and as far as you can see it is all the same till you reach the mountains. The Val d'Arno is so rich and prosperous, that it leaves no space for anything else. The Florentines would no doubt be far from pleased if they heard me say this, and they might have cause, for their city and its surroundings form a gem of loveliness. It is only my own individual taste which I am expressing.

We were at Petraja the other day,—a villa which was the Grand Duke's and is the King's; a dream of beauty it is;—terraces bordered by trellis-work, and orange-trees, with showers of roses, magnolias, and azaleas; a view over Florence, and away to the Carrara mountains; and behind the villa, a hill, planted with trees, commanding another view in a different direction, and having at its base one of those broad, solemn cypress avenues which form the contrast wanting to set off the glory of an Italian sky. Then, again, I have been to Careggi, to the house and into the room which Lorenzo the Magnificent occupied in his last illness, when Savonarola stood by his death-bed, and appealed for the freedom of Florence as the condition upon which he would grant him absolution, and Lorenzo turned his face to the wall and died unabsolved; and I have looked down into the well in the courtyard in which the physician who poisoned Lorenzo was thrown. But, strange to say, the place is not old and dreary, but as gay with paint and marble as English taste of the present day can make it, only there is something ghastly and ghostly in the memories which haunt it; and the long, narrow corridor running along the outside of the house, just under the roof, with the low rooms which open from it, the floors of which are so old as to be unsafe, remind one that the modern dress is only a *dress*, and that Careggi was really the place where the splendour and the guilt of the Medici were concentrated. A broad covered terrace or loggia opens from the rooms which Lorenzo last inhabited. It commands a splendid view over Florence; and there, no doubt, all the great men whom Lorenzo patronized often enjoyed themselves in the summer evenings. I was interested —very much interested—in looking at it. People belonging to that period became very real as one stood upon the precise spot where they must have congregated; but admiration or enthusiasm I felt none. The old walls of Etruscan Fiesole came home to me much more nearly, when we ascended the steep hill, a few miles out of Florence, to look at them. These small hills round Florence form one of its peculiarities. People speak of the Val d'Arno as if it was one valley, and Florence was situated in its centre; but this is not at all correct. There are really three divisions of the Val d'Arno, and Florence is built in the centre, with jagged hills of moderate height all round it; and it is from these that the beautiful views are obtained. Fiesole seems now almost a part of Florence. You drive to it along a high road, shut in by the garden walls of the Florentine villas; but you have to reach a height of a thousand feet above Florence before you stand on the site of the old Etruscan citadel, which is now a Franciscan convent. We were there only one evening, and that was not enough to see and understand it; for all the scattered bits of antiquity are so built into walls, and covered by churches and other buildings, that it is impossible to make them out without a good deal of searching. It does not do in these antiquarian visits to have a double object in view. If you are longing to look at the view, you are only bored with the antiquities; if, on the contrary, you really are bent upon learning all you can, you will do well to shut your eyes, in a great measure, to the scenery. I speak at least from personal experience.

Galileo's Tower is on another of the near Florentine hills. M—— and I made an expedition there the other evening. It is joined to some farm buildings now, and is left to its natural decay, which is all the better for those who have an interest in it. We found an open court and arcade, which must have been part of the dwelling-house, and by its side the old tower, ascended by a wooden staircase, and having little rooms opening out of it, from the top of which Galileo made his observations. It is a beautiful situation;—every height round Florence must command lovely views,—and the tower seems to sta[nd] lonely and apart, like the great astronomer himse[lf]. One thinks of the Medici family with even great[er] detestation when comparing their fame with his.

The modern Florentines appreciate their gre[at] men, for which we are bound to estimate them [in] proportion. Michael Angelo's house, the Palaz[z] Buonarotti, is kept in careful preservation. I don[']t know whether it most pleased or displeased me t[o] be told that his last male descendant has recentl[y] died. It seemed to bring Michael Angelo himsel[f] down to the present day more closely; but then i[t] took off somewhat of the shadowy awe with whic[h] names that have had great influence are invested[.] Anyhow, this last male descendant has acted mos[t] provokingly, and has left to the city a number o[f] manuscripts and letters, with a strict injunctio[n] that they are not to be published. The house i[s] too much "got up" with memorials and reminis[-] cences, and frescoes representing the chief event[s] in Michael Angelo's life, to be quite what on[e] wishes. There is a tiny cabinet containing hi[s] sword, and walking-sticks, and writing table, an[d] his slippers kept in a drawer; but I wish it ha[d] been possible to see them just where he lef[t] them. The removal of relics from their sur- roundings strikes one more and more as a mistake[,] though I suppose, generally speaking, an unavoidable one. Etruscan antiquities and Majolica ware are amongst the curiosities.

You see I am obliged to be discursive, for that is just what our days are. A list of our doings would be like the list of articles in a museum, without the advantage of orderly arrangement. We take two or three churches at a time, and frequently manage so as just to miss the right hour for seeing them. If we go too late, it is useless to attempt the pictures or sculpture, and we can only gain a general idea. The churches impress me more devotionally than the Roman churches; that is, I suppose, because the people themselves are more devout. We were wishing on Whit-Monday to see the Baptistry, and it was next to impossible. The whole of the floor of the great circular building was crowded with kneeling people. The Duomo, too, was well filled on that day. Both these buildings are of black and white marble in alternate layers, to which, as a matter of taste, I greatly object. The mixture destroys the light and shade; and besides, the lines become defaced and irregular from the effects of age and weather, and so the eye passes along a little distance, and is then stopped by the perception of something broken or ragged. Everything connected with the churches in Florence gives the idea of greater care and finish than in Rome. There is not indeed the same richness of material,—not the same amount of splendid marble columns, or magnificent altars, for instance,—and indeed the prevailing hues in the interior are dingy brown and white; but there are specimens of carving, and sculpture, and pictures, which would fill a gallery. I plead guilty to the very irreverent hope, that the pictures may do so at some not very distant day. Placed in churches, they are generally in such a bad light that it is difficult to see them, and impossible to enjoy them properly. The frescoes one can only sigh over. Masaccio, Ghirlandaio, Filippo and Filippino Lippi, Simone Memmi, and Taddeo Gaddi, are mythical names turned into household words, when one has made the circuit of Florentine churches and cloisters,— but there is not a work by any one of them which does not awaken a feeling of regret. They are all "dying by inches," and one looks at them as one does at beauty seen in wasting illness, with the thought,—if they are so lovely now, what would they be if their colours were fresh and bright? The carvings are very different, and they are certainly exquisite. I saw the other day a Tabernacle carved in bas-relief in the Church of Or San Michele, which, taken by itself, would make a city famous. One compartment represented an Angel announcing to the Blessed Virgin that she must die. The expression of the Virgin's face was like a new revelation of her mind. It seemed to describe all she might have felt when the great agony had passed, and the new joy had risen, and she had been left on earth waiting and longing for her blessedness. "Behold the handmaid of the Lord! be it unto me according to Thy Word," might be the motto for the scene described; only age and sorrow have left their traces upon the countenance, and there is eagerness in the awe, as well as surprise and humble acquiescence.

You will wonder, when I am writing about churches and pictures, that I say nothing of Fra Angelico; but that is because his paintings are for the most part in the Academia delle belle Arti, which has specimens of all the early Tuscan artists, and where, in fact, one can learn more about them than one can elsewhere. If persons do not *feel* Fra Angelico's paintings, they will be tolerably certain not to admire them at all. They are not, like Raphael's portraits, so perfect as to compel you to admire the picture, whatever you may think of the subject. His angels, for instance, are unquestionably quaint; and people might very likely object to the idea of an angel playing the violin. That is a kind of criticism which one does not attempt to argue against. It is quite true that we do not believe that angels ever did, or ever will, play the violin; and in the present day, such an angelic representation would be an offence against truth and reverence; but in Fra Angelico's age this material description of heavenly harmony was a natural expression of feeling, to which people were accustomed. It did not jar upon them; it was the language which they understood and appreciated; and Fra Angelico having learnt it himself, spoke it, of course, to others. The Pre-Raphaelite attempt to address the people of the nineteenth century in the language which suited the fourteenth, may be, and I suspect often is, a great mistake; but not to appreciate the spirit of the fourteenth because it does not suit the taste of the nineteenth, would seem to me a still greater. Angels are Fra Angelico's most perfect work; he wants strength for other subjects; and to admire the former you require to stand, and look, and think. It is a beauty which does not take you by storm, but steals into the heart,—just as one may believe that Fra Angelico's goodness did.

We have been to Santa Croce—the Westminster Abbey of Florence—where all the great men are buried. It is most disappointing; handsome indeed as regards design, but brown and white in colour, and indifferent in detail. The monuments are, like most monuments, in very bad taste; and though, as usual, there are good frescoes and various treasures of art, the church fails to excite awe or reverence as a whole. I can say nothing better of the celebrated Medicean Chapel, attached to the Church of San Lorenzo, which is as grand and rich as marble, and gold, and mosaic, can make it; in fact, just like the Medici themselves, as costly and pretentious, and as little impressive. One passes through it with perfect indifference, anxious only to see Michael Angelo's monument, with the statues of Dawn and Twilight, Night and Morning, which are in another chapel adjoining the church. It is quite curious to observe how completely the persons commemorated are lost in the fame of the sculptor. I should think scarcely one person in twenty, after seeing these monuments, remembers for whom they were erected; though Lorenzo, Catharine de Medici's father, is a most splendid figure,—grand and thoughtful, and fit, apparently, to have governed an empire; but his daughter's vices, and Michael Angelo's art, are his chief memorials in the eyes of his posterity. He is buried, with the rest of his family, under the weight of the very treasures of genius which they coveted for their earthly reward.

I shall have tired you with my description, as much as I am tired myself with so much sightseeing. Three weeks in Florence gives one only time for a mere sample of what there is to be visited. Happily, distances are less than at Rome;

but then again, unhappily, the objects of interest belong more to one class, so that one's impressions are more confused.

I ought to be able to tell you about the Misericordia,—a society established in Florence since 1244, in order to give aid when accidents happen, and to assist at funerals. It was begun by the porters belonging to a cloth manufactory, but now includes the chief persons in the city; even Grand Dukes have been members of it. We met a procession in the streets one day, but I had only a rapid glance of some persons dressed like monks, having their faces so completely covered that no features were to be recognised. They are excessively useful and energetic; people say that when the cholera was in Florence, in 1855, their services were invaluable. These are the things which make one pause so often, before passing a wholesale condemnation on the present Roman Catholic system.

Yours, &c. &c.

CHAPTER XXV.

Florence, May, 1861.

MY DEAR ——,

... You don't care for pictures, but you want to know something about the people and the religion. I can tell you nothing from my own knowledge, except as regards the services of the Chiesa Evangelica, which I have attended twice. You will be frightened, and think me a complete heretic; but I was determined to judge for myself about it. In itself, it is the very lowest of the low as regards government or discipline; indeed, a pamphlet which has been lent me, giving an account of its formation, plainly owns that it does not pretend to be a regular Church. It is simply the nucleus, out of which a Church may eventually be formed. It does not, therefore, join itself to the Waldensian or to any other Protestant body; on the contrary, it repudiates every idea of such union, and wishes to stand by itself—simply Italian. I need scarcely say that it recognises no priesthood, and, so far as I can learn, no dogmatic teaching, except the one article of Justification by Faith. The building in which the services that I attended were held, was, externally, like any other house; internally, it was a very decent little church, with a small nave, transepts, and chancel,—of course, not built for the purpose, but only adapted. There seems to be no secrecy or mystery in the proceedings; but there was just a look of surprise in the one or two poor people who were entering when our carriage drove up to the door, and I own I felt as if we were rather intruders. However, when a friend who was with me, and who lives in Florence, and knows the ways of the people, asked a few questions for information, we were evidently regarded as *sorelle*. We were well placed for observing the congregation, which was an interesting one: numbers of young men—tradesmen and mechanics, apparently; a few country people, chiefly peasant-women, and some young children; and two or three persons a few degrees above the working class,— amongst them Francesco Madiai, an honest, open-hearted, pleasant-tempered man, if one may judge from his countenance. They talked in an under tone, as people do when preparing to listen to a lecture, and there was a little moving and changing places when friends came in; but a great number had Bibles or Testaments open for reading.

The first service at which we were present was conducted by a Signor Magrini, who was in prison in the Grand Duke's time, and indeed spent ten years of his life between prison and exile. He looked and spoke like a gentleman, and had a sensible and benevolent face, betraying during his sermon a large amount of enthusiasm. The service began with a hymn, from a printed collection—it was sung seated; then followed a short prayer,—the people standing. The manner of the speaker was reverent, and his words were calm and simple; there was nothing in which one could not heartily join. The fifth chapter of the second of Corinthians was then read, and a sermon, or exposition of the chapter, followed. The first reference was to the Final Judgment, and I thought there might be an appeal to the consciences of the congregation, and some attempt to enlighten them as to the life which Christians ought to lead, and the sins which they ought not to commit;—but instead of this the preacher began a sketch of Biblical history, from the Creation to the Confusion of Tongues, deducing, as a conclusion, that as men in former days sought to save themselves from a second deluge by building the Tower of Babel, so now they thought to save themselves from judgment by a tower of works,—penances, prayers, church ceremonies, and submission to Papal ordinances. It was not by any means an un-eloquent or ineffective sermon, though, like most extempore effusions, too many lines of thought were entered upon without being carried out. The people were attentive and interested, and it was especially pleasant to see the young men evidently following what was said. The sketch of history, too, was graphic, and likely to be useful to ignorant persons; but I could not help thinking all the time that the preacher assumed, as the basis of his discourse, a fact of which he could in no way be cognisant,—that his congregation had a clear view of their duties, and a deep sense of their sinfulness. Looking at the standard of morality in Italy—and one may also say, in England—it is clear to me that people want quite as much to be shown that they are sinners, as to be assured that their sins are forgiven; and how this fact can be brought home to them without an explanation and enforcement of practical duties in detail, I don't understand.

After the sermon, the preacher announced to the *Fratelli* and *Sorelle* that a collection would be made for the poor people at Chiusi who had suffered from the earthquake. I observed a little hesitation as to who were to collect it. Two or three young men looked at each other, and at length stepped forward to offer their services. It was all singularly domestic and real; as complete a contrast to Romish ceremonies as could be imagined. The alms were collected in hats. About fifty francs I heard afterwards was the sum total, which, considering the size and condition of the congregation, was extremely good. A hymn and another prayer followed, and then we all dispersed.

The poor people who sat near us, and to whom Miss —— talked a little, were courteous, as all Italians of their class are; and more than that, there was an evident recognition of us as friends having the same hopes and interest. Whatever one may think of the doctrine or discipline of such a society, it is impossible not to be touched by the earnestness and simplicity of the individuals who compose it. One only longs so much that it should all be put on a safe and sound footing. I felt this longing, mingled with some fear, when I went to the service a second time. The preacher or *evangelista* then was a different person, a Signor Gualtiero. He was originally, I have been told, a *canonico*, who, having his eyes opened to Romish errors, fled to Turin. Great efforts were made by the priests to have him brought back for trial, but the Turin Government would not give him up. He returned at the time of the annexation, and now is a regularly appointed preacher of the Chiesa Evangelica. Florentine he certainly is—his dialect tells that. Any one who has ever heard the harsh guttural with which the Florentines murder their sweet-sounding language would recognise him at once. And he did not give me the impression of being such an educated person as Signor Magrini. Whether he was equally popular I cannot say, but the congregation was not quite so poor and attentive, and the numbers were fewer. His sermon was the counterpart of Signor Magrini's; he read to us a portion of the fifth chapter of St. John's Gospel, containing the warning of a future judgment, and deduced from it, that if the wicked were to be punished, then belief in a Saviour was necessary in order to escape the punishment.

As regarded Romanism, the burthen of the teaching in both cases was,—"the priests are men, they cannot save you; but you are wicked and you need a Saviour, therefore believe and you are saved;" and this repeated, again and again, under every form of enthusiastic phrase and gesture. I could not help thinking as I listened to Signor Gualtiero's eager voice, how easily the Chiesa Evangelica might be made the focus of political excitement, if the Government was not popular. As it is, *nostro Rè*, and his ministers, and parliament, were prayed for, and so far things are safe.

You will see from the tone of what I have said that I have no hope that the Chiesa Evangelica will be the regenerator of Italy. I did not expect it when I went, so I am not disappointed. I have talked to persons who see a good deal of the peasants, and can form a tolerably good opinion of the religious feeling of the people generally, and my impression is that, whatever may be the tottering condition of the Papacy, the *Church* in Italy has a stronger hold upon the sympathy and affection of the people than we are apt to imagine; and that any attempt at reformation in doctrine must, to be in the least permanently successful, be made through the appointed channels.

I will give you a few remarks as they have been made to me. I inquired of Miss —— about the religious feelings of the Contadine, whom she sees constantly. Her answer was, "I think a very pretty young girl who lives near us said what most of them would say, if you should ask for their confession of faith: 'I believe in our Saviour and the Madonna, and all the saints, and everybody in heaven; but I don't believe in the Pope very much, nor the priests, nor anybody in this world.'" Miss —— added, "That she had never yet known an unbeliever among the Contadine, and that they appeared to have a great faculty of separating between the priest and their religion." They are singularly ignorant of the elementary facts of sacred history. A poor but intelligent girl, who could read well, and was very devout, had a New Testament lent her to read whilst she was sitting to Miss —— for her portrait. At the end of the first sitting, she gave it as her opinion that "it was very interesting, and really appeared to be a good religious book!" She afterwards became very fond of it, and now and then addressed Miss —— in such words as— "O Signorina, this is pretty! Did you ever read how the wise men came to see the little Gesù Bambino?" or, "O Signorina, did you ever hear about Peter and the cock crowing? That is a beautiful story!" "It is very strange," she said once, "I have read the Via del Paradiso, and the Office of the Madonna, and all the prayers of the Church, and I never saw this beautiful book before." Miss —— told her that many good people had found great consolation in reading it. "Yes," she said, "that is the word, consolation; that is what one feels in reading it."

This girl was a strict Roman Catholic, and had not the slightest idea what she was reading; neither did my friend make any attempt to convert her, as it is called. She never railed against the priests, or even discussed any particular form of Roman Catholic error. She simply set before her facts acknowledged, and truths held by her Church, though they lie buried beneath a load of superstition; and the simple, untrained mind recognised, and was influenced by them at once. And this (I really fear to give an opinion upon such a subject) certainly seems to me to give somewhat of a clue to the means by which, if there is to be a safe and sure Reformation in Italy, it must be brought about; namely, not by destroying, but building up; not by attacking error, but preaching and upholding truth. I know there must be enormous difficulties in the way,—yet I cannot but think that if, instead of crying out against the worship of the Virgin, a few Roman Catholic priests, whose eyes are opened, could be induced to bring forward and dwell upon the all-sufficient Atonement and Mediation of Christ, they would by degrees wean their people from a false doctrine without that terrible risk of unsettling the foundations of faith, which must always exist in any attempt at controversy.

And the same may be said of other doctrines. There is a germ of truth at the root of almost every Romish error—why not take advantage of it? The moment you attempt controversy you put the mind into an undevotional, antagonistic state—the very opposite of that necessary for the reception of Christian truth. If St. Paul, in preaching to the Athenians, recognised the truths of Heathenism, surely we must and ought to recognise the truths of Romanism. And, as it appears to me, it would be worse than vain to attempt to destroy all the outward forms of Romanism; they have become a part of the people's daily life; they are mixed up with all their joys, their sorrows, and their needs. And to

a southern temperament they would seem to be an
absolute necessity. Southern nations must, in a
measure, walk by sight; they must have ceremonies,
and brightness, and show, and variety;—their religion must be demonstrative, or it will cease to be
religion at all. We may enlighten them as to our
own belief, and explain to them the meaning of our
Church services; and so far we may do good by
enlarging their minds, and leading them to distinguish essentials from non-essentials; but they will
never be brought to worship after our fashion, any
more than they will be induced to live after it. It
is this, amongst other reasons, which makes me look
with doubt upon all foreign movements for what is
called the conversion of Italy. I do not believe we
understand the habits and feelings of Italians sufficiently to know what we are about when we meddle
with their religion *controversially;* and, as I said
before, I cannot but think that whatever may be the
distrust with which individual priests are regarded,
the masses of the people still look to them, as a body,
with so much traditional respect, that any movement
to be really effective must originate with them. For
that we must wait God's time. As a friend of mine
said to me the other day: " It is a Savonarola who is
needed;" and it may be that before long a Savonarola
will arise. All this is very superficial. I merely give
you the results of what I gather from my own hasty

observations, and a few conversations with people who know more.

The Contadine must be very winning in their simplicity. I received the other day quite a touching account of a young girl, who had lost her mother when she was a child, and had been in consequence left a good deal to herself. She said once to Miss ——, "It must be very easy for a Signorina to be good. You are taken so much care of; you never hear or see anything there is any harm in. But I have to go to Florence, and about all the streets by myself, and I hear certain things—it is hard to keep them out of my mind afterwards; but if I ever think of them I begin to sing, and then they go away." And then she told Miss —— the following legend:— "When our Saviour was on earth," she said, "He passed by a field where two girls were at work, and they were singing very gaily, and He stood still a little to hear them. Afterwards He passed a convent, but He did not stop there. And a Saint, or whoever it was that was with Him, asked Him how it could be that He had stopped to hear those two common Contadine, and had not stood still at all when He passed the convent where so many pious nuns were living. And He said it was because He knew that when the two girls were singing they could have no room for bad thoughts; but as for the nuns, they were all silent, and they might be thinking of anything!"

There is a world of wisdom in the legend, if one would but profit by it. Singing seems the one favourite amusement of the peasants. They delight in what they call *stornelli*—which are little love or war songs,—often in part improvised, but each one ending with the same chorus. I suspect Victor Emmanuel owes no small portion of his success to the *stornelli*. They are an exemplification of the sayings of—I forget whom,— "Give me the making of the ballads of a country, and I care not who makes its laws." Hearing Miss —— sing one of them—which was popular after the peace of Vilafranca—it was scarcely possible to help being excited and joining in the chorus,

"Lascia l' andar, che volontario l' è
Vittorio Emanuele si vuol per nostro Rè."

One last word, and then really I will end. I asked Miss —— what the poor people thought of Baron Ricasoli, and she gave me in reply the remarks she had heard. "Il Bettino," they said, "was such a good man—so much to be depended on, and so kind and civil to the poor!" "There is a good gentleman," said a poor girl one day, after Ricasoli had passed the window. "I would not be afraid of him; one knows that he is good when one looks at him."

Very small testimony to a man's worth these are,—yet I should think they would be prized. Report says that Baron Ricasoli is a Protestant; but, so far as I can learn, this only means that he is a Catholic, and not a Romanist. I suppose the report originated from the fact, that application was made to him to put a stop to the meetings of the Chiesa Evangelica, when he refused, saying, that although he was a Roman Catholic himself, he could not interfere with other persons' liberty of conscience. Yours, &c. &c.

Florence, May 31*st*, 1861.

My dear ——,

We are preparing for our journey on Monday by seeing, if not all we have left unseen, yet, at least, all which we had made up our minds we would see. I shall regret Florence for the pictures, and I shall keep it in tender remembrance for its beauty; but I could never feel for it as I do for Rome. It has too much of the tone of a modern city to take the same deep hold of one's affections. But I don't mean to be ungrateful, and one ought to remember the saying, "comparisons are odious,"—only I think I should have felt more for it if I had seen it first. We hope to go to Pisa on Monday, starting by the railway at four o'clock in the afternoon. There we must see the Duomo and the Campo Santo, and sleep; and at six o'clock the next day we shall, if nothing should interfere, set off for Genoa by *Vetturino.* From Genoa we purpose going to Turin by the railway. I am looking forward to the drive from Spezzia to Genoa, which, they say, is enchantingly lovely.

And now for our doings here. This last week we have been searching after modern art. We were at Powers' studio on Wednesday, and I must acknowledge myself considerably disappointed. He seems to have but one idea of beauty, which is constantly repeated. We were shown a statue of America—not to be sent yet because of the disturbances. The face is beautiful,—but wanting in strength of expression. Nothing I saw gave me the idea of any great original genius—anything which would go down to posterity. A cast of the Rape of Proserpine in the studio of Fedi, an Italian artist, was to me infinitely more indicative of great talent. The figures indeed are confessed to be so fine, that they are to be placed in the Loggia.

Certainly the Italians seem to have that in them which no other nation can attain. I saw the other day in the Palazzo Pitti two marvellously life—and death—like statues of Cain and Abel, by Dupré, a modern sculptor. The story connected with them is singular. Dupré is a Sienese, the son of a woodcarver. As a child, he amused himself with making mud figures in the streets of Siena,—but he had no instruction in the art of sculpture. He married very young, and then, encouraged by his wife, made a plaster figure of a dead Abel. When it was finished, the artists said it was so like nature that no untaught genius could have produced it;—the sculptor must have actually murdered a man and taken a cast of the head! The Grand Duke, though his firm friend, said, that under such an accusation he could do nothing for him ; but if he would model a "Cain" for the next year's Exhibition, leaving his studio open day and night, that all might know it was his own work, he would take him by the hand. The "Cain" was produced; and Dupré, after some years of hard struggle, is now one of the first of modern sculptors.

One morning we spent at the Uffizi, which contains a quantity of rare things besides the pictures and statues;—chiefly we devoted ourselves to the Cameos and Medals in the Cabinet of Gems. They can only be seen by special permission, and even with this precaution a great number were stolen not long ago. There are besides a great number of original drawings by the great Masters, and a collection of Bronzes, which are no doubt extremely fine, but which never give me much real pleasure—one misses so much the vivid light and shade of marble. Then there is a rich collection of Majolica ware; which is another specimen of art that I can always see without coveting. Many of the dishes in the Uffizi were copies of Raphael's pictures—extremely curious, but not in the least awakening the feeling of the pictures themselves. I never understood before the difference between Majolica and Palissy ware. In the latter, the pattern or picture is raised; in the former it is not. There is besides, I believe, a kind of German porcelain of the same character, which is superior in material, but inferior in enamel. It is a comfort when one sees all these rare things to find how much there is in the world which one does *not wish* to possess.

We have been to the Mosaic manufactory. The flowers and figures are formed from real stones inlaid, and this makes them more expensive and more enduring than Roman Mosaic. The latter, I think, strikes me as more ingenious and open to variety; but there are some specimens of Florentine work which nothing Roman can equal.

The pictures grow upon me; and now that I am going away, I long for some of the copies which I despised when I could have the original. There is an Italian here, Signor Rocchi, who copies charmingly. His Fra Angelico Angels are really perfect. Even outlines of the great pictures one should be thankful for at a distance. We have made acquaintance with an old man who devotes himself to this, and nothing else. He traces sometimes from the pictures themselves,—but you can procure outlines of any particular figures by ordering them; and so also Signor Rocchi will copy any one figure which may strike the fancy. This would be my pleasure. It so often happens that a picture, which one does not care for as a whole, contains some one face or form which one delights in. Especially is this the case in what may be called joint pictures, in which perhaps Perugino or Raphael painted one or two figures, and left the rest for an inferior hand. It is curious to watch the different trades which are indigenous to different places. This copying is as much a business in Florence as the trade of a blacksmith is in a country village in England. I should like to know how far it really refines the mind; but that is a question which one might ask about all art. Biographies of great artists give such singular revelations of the very earthly life, which is quite compatible with the most vivid imagination of spiritual beauty.

Yours, &c. &c.

CHAPTER XXVI.

[*Bugiasta or Pugiasta, (or something of the kind; but we can't quite make out where we are, only it is half-way between Spezzia and Sestri, and on the road to Genoa.*)

June 5th, 1861.

My dear ——,

This is where we are;—how we are, and what we are doing, is another question. At this moment we are occupying a dirty room, in a dirty house, in a dirty street, in a dirty village amongst the mountains. Mrs —— is seated in a three-legged armchair, which has subsided towards the ground on the left, and offers, consequently, rather an uneasy position. L—— sitting, leaning against the wall near the door, has Butt's "History of Italy" in her hand, and some cold tongue and bread by her side; this being a token that she cannot wait for our dinner at half-past eleven, but must needs have support at half-past ten. M—— places an Italian grammar on her lap for show, and reads an Italian play for her amusement. I—with a newspaper carefully spread out on the table, that I might not be obliged to touch anything so far from clean, and being well provided with writing materials—am, as you may have already perceived, writing a letter home. Josephine and Giuseppe are wandering amongst some of the hidden recesses of the mansion, preparing, as we hope, a meal which is to be neither breakfast, nor dinner, but may be eaten about half-past eleven; and at one, I suppose we shall find ourselves packed into the carriage again, and on our way to Sestri, where we are to sleep to-night.

I wrote last as we were about to leave Florence. We were off by the railway at four o'clock, and reached Pisa about six, in time to have rather a hurried view of the Duomo, the Baptistery, the Leaning Tower, and the Campo Santo.

They all stand together on an open green space, rather outside the town. Both the Duomo and the Baptistery are black and white, which, as I said in a former letter, I never can thoroughly admire. There are very beautiful things in the Duomo in the way of pictures and carving, but nothing that struck me like the richness of the interior of the Baptistery. It is circular, like all baptisteries, and empty, except for the colonnade which is carried round it, the large font in the centre, enclosed by a marble screen of the most exquisite carving I ever saw, and Nicolo Pisano's wonderful pulpit, supported by columns resting upon animals, and sculptured with the most elaborate bas-relief.

The Campo Santo infinitely surpassed my expectations. After the hideous church architecture of Southern Italy, which, to me, is the most unecclesiastical of all things, the sight of the rich Gothic tracery of the cloisters was a perfect joy. The green grass in the centre, which covers the earth brought from Mount Calvary, is well kept, the shrubs flourish, and there is an air of brightness and delicate beauty about the whole which is as unlike as possible to my solemn imaginings, and the sombre half-realities of photographs. Sunshine is one thing which photographs never scarcely give, and though we saw the Campo Santo late in the evening, I should still instinctively associate sunshine with it,—that gleaming, dazzling sunshine which falls in long lines through mullions and arches, and makes the shadows of carved tracery dance upon the pavement. The cloisters are filled with monuments and inscriptions, and the floor is paved with tombs. I looked with considerable interest at a Greek sarcophagus, converted into a Christian tomb, and containing the body of the Countess Beatrice, the mother of the Countess Matilda. It carried one back so vividly to the establishment of that Papal temporal dominion which has influenced Europe for centuries, and of which, perhaps, we are destined to see the end. The walls of the Campo Santo are covered with the frescoes, which one knows so well by name. They are faded of course, and very strange, and require a great deal of study; but Orgagna's " Triumph of Death," and " The Last Judgment," have volumes of thought, and teaching, and warning in them; they are, in Art, very like what the " Pilgrim's Progress " is in Literature,—most quaint, and undoubtedly faulty, but so striking and so real, that you feel your business is not to criticise but to learn from them.

As a token of the present unity of Italy, the Pisans have hung up in the Campo Santo some portions of the chains of the Port of Pisa, taken by the Genocse in the fourteenth century, and now restored as the pledge and sign of a new era (so the inscription says) in the nineteenth. Does not this bring dates and events curiously near together?

Pisa itself is a rather dull, rather handsome town, with a decided air of decayed gentility. We were in a hotel near the Arno, which was comfortable enough; but along the banks of the river, and in the narrow street before my room, the people kept up all night a noise, which it is impossible to describe. One dreadful old man, with a thundering voice, seemed to occupy himself with shouting directly under my window, and at the same time rolling stones into a cart; and this employment (whatever it might be) he persisted in till two

o'clock in the morning. Little enough sleep had
I,—though we went to bed about nine. At half-
past four I was called, and in a state of weariness
and fatigue, which excited my utmost pity for
myself, I got up. We started soon after six,
M—— and myself on the outside seat. What with
pleasant conversation, the reading of "Rienzi"
and the newspaper, and occasional little naps, I
managed to spend a very agreeable day, in spite
of some heat and a good deal of fatigue. We had
a bright though not exciting country the whole
way—groves of olives, with vines twined amongst
them, for a foreground, and in the rear the jagged
outlines of the Carrara mountains. About six we
made a sudden turn amongst the hills and came in
sight of Spezzia and the sea;—a view so perfect in
its loveliness, that I longed for you from the first
moment I saw it till I lost sight of it this morning.
The town is small, and, though very quiet, has
a regular watering-place look. It lies at the foot
of the mountains, and close on the shore. Our
hotel, the Croce di Malta, fronted the bay; and
though I was very tired, and had an uncomfortable
cold, it was an enchantment to lean upon the
marble balustrade in front of the window, and
look out upon the calm sea, and the mountains
which gather round the bay,—the nearer hills
covered with olives and chestnuts, and the more

distant, grey, and jagged, and mysterious, as mountains always are. Shelley was drowned in the Bay of Spezzia, and from our window we could see the jutting point behind which the accident happened. I have no feeling for Shelley, except a kind of perplexed admiration, which is rather chilling than the reverse; but the spot has become in a measure historical, at least as regards poetry. I think I could feel more for him if people were not so inclined to make his genius an excuse for his principles,—a doctrine I never can admit.

We all went to bed very early, and were off again this morning at seven. A grey day it has been, and there is now a little threatening of rain; but we have, nevertheless, had a most enjoyable morning. After all, there is nothing to me like the excitement of scenery, and to look down upon the Bay of Spezzia from the mountains, up which our road took us, was a delight not to be forgotten. I did not imagine before how lovely olive-groves could be; but here the peculiar soft greyish-green, which is rather sombre in itself, is brightened by the vines which the peasants twine from tree to tree, and which hang in festoons over the little plots of wheat, amongst which the olives are planted. These olives and vines, with chestnuts, clothe the sides of the steep hills which descend to the Bay.

Point after point juts out into the sea, and the stern grey mountains in the distance rise,—first one, then another,—assuming different outlines, and coming out more or less distinctly, and peeping between the depressions of the lower range, till the effect is magical in its beauty. To complete our good fortune to-day we met winding along the mountain road, a troop of Sardinian cavalry, well mounted and equipped; each horseman bearing his purple pennon at the end of his lance. L—— called out, "*Viva!*" and was greeted with "*Viva!*" in return; and Josephine, who is a thorough Italian, asked if they were going to Rome; to which, of course, they replied, "Yes;" for every Italian soldier thinks he is going, or shall go, to Rome.

Ruta, June 6th.—Another hitherto unknown place between Sestri and Genoa. As we are waiting for our luncheon I must finish my letter. At Sestri, where we slept last night, I saw nothing more than a hotel on the shore, with a few cottages about it. We had a wet evening after our grey day, and were dreading rain this morning, but most happily the clouds have all cleared away. This Gulf of Genoa, round which our road has wound all the morning, is a perfect dreamland; and in spite of fatigue, and a tendency to headache, which has just blunted the edge of my pleasure, the journey is one which

I would not but have taken for worlds, as the saying is. We are resting to-day, as we did yesterday, in a room far from clean, in which painted walls and ceilings atone but indifferently for dirty brick floors; but when I look out of the window I can see the wooded sides of the steep mountains, the Mediterranean—fabulously blue—at their base;— the sharp angles of the hills projecting into the Bay, and little white towns, with their tall Campaniles, dotted about on the shore, and on the heights above: in the far distance, the villas of Genoa; and away, beyond—only half real in their misty grandeur—the long line of the Alps, with the snow-peaks which rise above Turin. This is the kind of view we have had all the morning, for the road has carried us just above the sea nearly the whole way; only once or twice we turned inland for a short space, and then were amongst hills and chestnut groves, with all imaginable colours and forms of beauty, such as belong to this mountain country. For once I have seen what Mediterranean blue can be. I laughed this morning at Sestri when I looked at the painted ceiling of our room, and saw what the painter wished to represent as sea—the colour seemed an absurdity, but I really scarcely think it is so now. And there is one tint so wonderfully beautiful!—the greenish-blue, which is seen amongst the olive leaves when you look down the perpendicular sides of the mountains upon the sea, which washes their very base. But I am not a convert to a tideless sea, at least for a continuance. I want nothing changed *now* as I am passing through the country; but, if I lived here, I feel there would be times when I should yearn for a smooth stretch of sand, and the interest of a flowing or a receding tide. Unchangeableness upon earth, in any form, is oppressive. It is not a type which has any antitype in our own nature.

Turin, June 7th.—I left off yesterday with my thoughts full of olive groves and Mediterranean blue. To-day I am writing from the Hôtel de l'Europe, at Turin; and the one idea in my mind is Count Cavour's funeral. The news of his death came upon us this morning at Genoa, like a thunderbolt. Travelling as we were, we had scarcely heard he was ill; and though all Genoa knew what had happened yesterday, we saw no one who was likely to mention it to us. I suppose we were too much occupied in settling ourselves in the very noisy hotel after our *Vetturino* journey, and too anxious to make the most of our short time by driving round the town to show M——, who had never been at Genoa before, the Public Gardens, and the Churches, and the Harbour, to have any thought, or to ask any questions about other things.

This morning we were in the usual bustle of preparation for a railway journey, besides receiving some friends who had just landed from Leghorn after a very stormy passage, when this astounding and overwhelming piece of news came upon us. Certainly no foreign political event ever came home to me in the same way. It was an actual personal sorrow, and so it is still; one can scarcely tell why,—only being in Italy has made Italian interests become so real. We had not the least idea when the funeral would be, and we felt sure that we could not see the Parliament sitting, which was what we most wished for; but we still thought it better to come on to Turin, so we started as we had intended, and then learnt by accident from a gentleman in the railway carriage that the Count was to be buried this afternoon, at six o'clock. Our friend was a Sicilian, a friend of Garibaldi, and known to Cavour, and it was immensely interesting to hear him talk. We made acquaintance at first through a very engaging little girl whom he had with him,—a child of about seven, and whom we assisted with needles and thread when she wanted to work. This won the father's heart, and he became very communicative, pouring forth a flood of mingled French and Italian, so rapidly, that I don't think he knew himself which language he was talking. I listened to him with great interest as probably a specimen of the ultra-Garibaldi Italian character—very excitable, very vague, both in politics and religion, and a good deal inclined to egotism and boastfulness, (though this is by no means a personal characteristic of Garibaldi,) not refined, yet withal generous in tone, and tender and thoughtful to the little one who claimed his protection. He spoke delightfully of Cavour in a political point of view, though he said that Italy had now advanced too far for the death of even such a man to stop its progress. Ricasoli (the late Governor of Florence) is now, he said, the man to whom people turn. Ratazzi does not understand the Emperor. He showed this when he was Minister after the Peace of Villafranca. He did what the Emperor said, and could not understand that his words were always to be interpreted in precisely the contrary sense. Count Cavour's habits of life were, as we are told, sufficient in themselves to kill him. He worked from six in the morning till twelve at night,—ate enormously, and never walked except from his house to the Chambers. The king was with him continually during his illness, sitting by his bedside for four hours at a time. At the last Cavour was unconscious, and the physicians were obliged to tell the king that he would do better to leave him, since he was only suffering himself without doing any good. The king left him at six, and at seven Cavour was dead.

We came into Turin about two o'clock. Passing through the streets, one could have said, " that there was not a house in which there was not *one* dead. " We had written for apartments at the Hôtel de l'Europe, and front rooms were secured to us, so that we had the best possible position for seeing the procession, which passed from the Piazza di S. Carlo to the Piazza Reale—our street uniting the two. Our balconies were draped with white and black hangings, and so indeed were the balconies of all the houses. The first sound of the procession which we heard, after waiting in expectation for hours, was the dull tramp of a large body of soldiers, who marched up the street and stationed themselves directly in front of our windows; then a few officers, in splendid uniforms, rode up slowly, followed by other troops, and so they moved on into the Piazza Reale; and the street was filled with more and more. A crowd accompanied them, but perfectly quiet and sorrowful. There may have been grander processions,—though there could scarcely be more magnificent uniforms and trappings than those of the Sardinian cavalry, or finer soldiers than the troops which passed under our window,—but a more touching sight it would be impossible to imagine. When, after the long lines

x

of soldiers, and the procession of priests, the hearse came in sight, with the royal servants in their scarlet liveries attending it, and the train of parliamentary deputies following; and the people threw flowers from the windows, and one saw them carefully gathered up and placed upon the bier, which was open to view,—I do not think even a stoic could have looked on unmoved. But more striking even than this was the crowd of persons of all classes behind,—artisans, men in blouses and working dresses, Garibaldi's soldiers in their red jackets, all walking with that peculiar, solemn, funeral step which one so rarely sees, and making one feel that their whole heart was bent upon the one object of doing honour to Cavour. Rain poured the whole time, and so far there was a sense of discomfort and annoyance to distract our thoughts; but it was more for others than for ourselves. I could not help feeling for the soldiers, as, waiting for the hearse, they stood lining the streets, with the rain pouring down upon them; whilst the brilliant red and silver uniforms of the cavalry officers looked as if they could never have been intended for anything but sunshine. The procession entered the Piazza Reale, and passed round the old Madama Palace, which stands in the centre, and then we lost sight of it; but I believe it proceeded to a church very near Count Cavour's Palace, and where he is to be laid for the present; though ultimately, at his own request, he is to be buried at some place of his own in the country.

Through all this honour and fame, the chief thought in one's mind is, and must be, what he was personally and privately. Our friend of the railway spoke of him as a man whose faith was expediency,—who was what he thought it most advisable to be. Our waiter said that he knew he was dying, and that a Capuchin monk was with him constantly. I don't particularly respect Capuchin monks, but then I have only seen them as they haunt the streets, with their brown cloaks, and long dirty beards, and low faces. One thing I know, that after being in Italy, and seeing what Romanism is here, it is far more easy to excuse a man for being a Rationalist than when one has only had an opportunity of comparing Rationalism and the Church of England.   Yours, &c. &c.

P.S.—The way the people speak of their loss makes one feel deeply how great it is. Between two and three thousand persons were waiting before Cavour's house the day previous to his death, to hear tidings of him; and it is said that the night he died thousands never went to bed, from their anxiety to know what his state was. He was very rich, but gave away a great deal in charity. His money goes to a young Marquis de Cavour, his nephew.

CHAPTER XXVII.

TURIN touched me with a *present* interest more deeply than any place I ever saw;—somewhat of this must, of course, be attributed to the circumstances under which we visited it. Even if antagonistic to Count Cavour's policy, it would have been impossible not to feel his death. But the real truth is, that the condition of Italy at this moment tends to shake the foundation of all political theories by the "inexorable logic of facts." You cannot live amongst the Italians and wish that the Austrians should bear rule over them; you cannot see an effort made to shake off that rule, without sympathising with it. And Turin is the very heart—it contains the life-blood of Italy, and the pulsation is felt at each turn. To attempt to restore Italy is like attempting to restore the circulation of a man who has been nearly drowned. In the extremities—in Rome and at Naples—it would seem a hopeless effort; at Florence there is life, but it is uncertain; powers are at work there which may again paralyse the newly-restored animation, and there are times when one cannot but fear for the event; but at Turin, one has no fear, no doubt;—the energy is so strong, the spirit so earnest, it must in the end gain the victory over the moral death which is striving so hard for the conquest of the country.

It is this spirit which has imprinted itself upon the city. Turin, I had been told, was quite modern; therefore, quite uninteresting. I found it completely the reverse. Like the government of the country, it has a modern form, but its spirit is that of a grave and heart-stirring antiquity. The streets are ornamented with arcades, and remarkably regular; the piazzas are handsome; there are good shops, pleasant public walks, excellent hotels; —so far, it might be Paris. But the type of Turin is the old Madama Palace, in the centre of the Piazza Reale, which, on one side, has a regular Grecian façade, with composite columns, and pilasters, architraves, cornices, statues,—and all things in due architectural proportion; whilst on the other, are quaint octangular towers, little wooden balconies, loophole windows, and heavy doorways, which belong to the Middle Ages.

We spent a morning in seeing the Gallery of paintings in the Palazzo Madama, and in going over the modern Royal Palace, which occupies one side of the great Piazza. The King was not there; he was at a hunting-seat, where he had shut himself up ever since Count Cavour's death.

The Turin pictures are not, I believe, particularly celebrated; but I learnt from them to admire Gaudenzio Ferrari, a Lombard artist, whose works are not very numerous in other places. There is a picture of his in the Brera, at Milan, of the Martyrdom of St. Catharine, which ever since I first saw it, in 1851, has held a first place in my memory; the face of St. Catharine expresses such marvellous peace in suffering. And now, at Turin, I saw others, not I think quite equal, but certainly more than usually beautiful in colouring and design. There were some Vandykes also, " Children of the House of Savoy,"—little round faces ready for a game of play, but royally "got up," and very properly decorous, and looking as living and real as all Vandyke's pictures do; besides two first-rate Rembrandts—a Head of an old Rabbi, and a Burgomaster, with a good number of others, more or less interesting, but not gaining for themselves a very definite place in one's recollections.

Perhaps I cared less for them because I cared so much for other things in the Palace,—the Museum especially, which has a collection of modern treasures that have already acquired the immortality of history. Not that these are what people generally go to see in the Museum at Turin. It is the armoury which is considered the great attraction, being considered the best in Europe; but I confess that I turned with indifference from the splendid horses, covered with the skins of the real animals, who had belonged to celebrated persons; and thought but little of Charles the Fifth's saddle, and was not at all excited by seeing Napoleon's sword, or even a lock of his hair kept as a relic. What I really cared for were the presents sent to Victor Emmanuel from the different Italian States and cities, since their annexation. Amongst them was a magnificent saddle, with silver stirrups, the gift of the Æmilian provinces, and used once when the King entered Bologna; an Album, with a case of carved coral, from Naples; another, with a velvet case studded with diamonds, from the Florentine ladies; a silver chain-shirt, from Milan; a crown of gold leaves, given by Turin when the King took the title of King of Italy; with the sword from Rome, which caused the exile of Castellani.

Banners from Milan and Gaeta, and relics of the war of 1848, including Austrian flags, were all carefully kept, and exhibited by a grave, gentlemanlike man, whose manner exhibited the deepest dejection, and whose eyes were glistening with tears as we alluded to the country's loss. "It was," he said, "a *colpo mortale* for the King,—and there was no one to take Count Cavour's place. Ricasoli had refused; he dreaded the responsibility."

(Such was the report at first, and I believe it was true.) This last intelligence was evidently, to him, the climax of disheartening disappointment, and it could not but be so in a measure to us. It seemed as though the very gifts at which we were looking might, before long, be violently taken away; for no one could at that time help dreading lest Austria should take advantage of the moment of Italy's weakness to make another effort for the recovery of her power,—or at least for the carrying out of the treaty of Villafranca.

We left the Armoury and went to the Palace. It was all bright with gilt and crimson. But we walked through it with a heart-ache. The King's loss, as well as that of the country, had become a deep reality,—and we felt his loneliness all the more from the reminiscences of his family sorrows. The room in which his mother, Maria Teresa, died, was pointed out to us, with another, which had been occupied by his wife, Maria Adelaide. To the latter apartment a small movable cabinet was attached, so contrived as to let down into the garden. It was made especially for the Queen during her illness, that she might reach the open air without difficulty. I believe there is no doubt that Victor Emmanuel was devotedly attached to his wife; and this genuine affection, joined with his truth and courage, are, no doubt, the qualities which endear him to his people, and make them overlook faults that are really open to grave censure.

The Royal Chapel which joins the Palace, and opens into the Cathedral, has another association with the late Queen. It is in itself very striking, being built of black marble and bronze; and it is consecrated, I believe, in the eyes of Romanists, by one of those painful legendary relics which one always wishes to put aside and forget; but what interested us were the monuments of some of the Dukes and Kings of Savoy, placed round it in four recesses, whilst a fifth was occupied by the sitting statue of Maria Adelaide. The recess had once been Victor Emmanuel's seat when he attended Mass in the Cathedral; but when his wife died he placed her statue there, and has never, so we were told, been present in the chapel at any service since.

We saw also that morning the two Chambers in which the Parliament meet. The Upper Chamber, which in itself is in no way remarkable, had a special interest, as it was there that Count Cavour made his last speech. The place where he always sat was pointed out to us,—it had already become sacred in the eyes of Italians. When we arrived at Turin, we had no hope of being present at a sitting of Parliament; but our Sicilian friend, who had promised to call upon us, came, after our visit to the Palace, to bring us tickets of admission for Monday,—the Chambers having only been prorogued till then. His little girl was with him, and his brother. He was as voluble and excited as before, and produced a novel which he had lately written, and which he begged us to accept. A most remarkable production it was, as I found when I read it!—the Pope, Antonelli, and Lamoricière, being brought in by name, and made to take part in a plot of atrocious and not very readable wickedness. I should like to know whether there was the slightest foundation for the facts confidently alluded to, especially with regard to Lamoricière's character; if not, a more astonishing libel could scarcely be imagined. But my own experience of the gentleman's powers of large deductions from slight premises would make me listen with considerable doubt to his assertions. We talked of England and America. He was very sympathetic with the latter,—not at all so with the former. I tried to impress upon him that I was an Englishwoman; but I am not sure whether he distinguished me from my friends. Certainly he did not prove it by his conversation. Something was said about the English Church, and he launched forth into a satire upon our Bishops. "He had seen a Bishop, in Ireland, going to a dinner party on a Friday, with a wife and daughter handsomely dressed, and quite *decolletées*. If he might have a large income, and a fine house, and a wife and daughters, he would not object to being a bishop himself." I could say nothing, and he went on:—" As for the English, eating and drinking was their delight. He had been at a party (I did not understand where) connected with a society of Freemasons; the gentlemen drank till they fell under the table." I looked at one of my friends in surprise,—but I really had no resource except silence. He saw the expression of my face, and stopped. " Surely he was correct. I could not disavow such habits?" I could only reply, "That they were not those of good society." "Oh!" he exclaimed, " very likely,— the English of the better class, who come abroad, and see how different the continental nations are, go home and wish to imitate us;—no doubt that is the case."

Such experiences of misconception do not so much make one angry as thoughtful and cautious. If others can be betrayed into such grievous and uncharitable blunders by hasty conclusions and reckless assertions, why may not the same happen in one's own case? After thinking over a conversation of this kind, I could almost make up my mind never again to give an opinion upon the character or conduct of either nations or individuals.

CHAPTER XXVIII.

Turin, June 10th, 1861.

My dear——,

Though I wrote so lately, I must add something more to-day, for we have been to the Superga —a great Church and Convent, on the top of what may almost be called a mountain, about four miles out of Turin, and which is one of a range of sharp-pointed, wooded hills, rising to the height of twelve or fifteen hundred feet, in the immediate vicinity of the town. They give variety and picturesqueness to all the views, and with the river Po, which flows through Turin, form a most beautiful foreground to the grand line of the snowy Alps beyond. I had no idea indeed how beautiful Turin was till I came here. People have always cried it down as being such a tame, modern city, but it has great attractions, and I should like nothing better than to stay longer and thoroughly explore the neighbourhood. The Superga hill is so steep, that we were obliged to have four horses to drag us up. The church on the summit has been the burial-place of many of the Royal Family of Piedmont since the days of Victor Amadeus, who, when about to engage in a battle with the French in the time of Louis the Fourteenth, made a vow that, if he were victorious, he would build a church, dedicated to the Blessed Virgin, on the top of the mountain from which he looked down upon his enemy's forces and his own threatened capital. The victory was gained, and the church was built within twenty years after, and a very Italian building it is; cupola, portico, magnificent marble columns, statues, bas-reliefs, and monuments, in deplorably bad taste. But the view which it commands, and the associations which it awakens, make one overlook any defects in the building or its adjuncts.

My rainy fate followed me, and going up the hill we had one of the fiercest hail-storms, with thunder and lightning, that I ever remember. (I see Murray says that Turin hail-storms are so celebrated, that an insurance office has been established to guard the cultivators of lands from the risk of the destruction of their crops in consequence;—so far I ought not to complain of having been favoured with a local personal experience.) We could only cower under the hood of the carriage—four of us—and shelter ourselves as best we might. The storm had abated when we reached the top, and the outlines of the mountains were visible; but I can scarcely say that I *saw* the view, though I have a very good idea of it.

From the broad flight of steps in front of the church we could look over the great plain between Turin and the Alps—rich, and bright, and cultivated; and rising directly from it was the long line of magnificent mountains from Monte Viso to (I think) the Splugen, with opening valleys, into which the sun's rays were streaming through the mist. Then, on the other side, we had the plains of Lombardy, from Genoa and the Mediterranean to Marengo and Milan, with a steep foreground of wooded mountain sides and deep ravines.

This was the external view. Internally, as I said before, there was little to please in point of taste; but the associations of the Royal Family were indescribably touching. The Monastery (or I believe, more strictly speaking, the College attached to the Church) has been suppressed—only two priests being allowed to remain in it, so we were allowed to walk through the refectory, and the hall, which made me think of the common-rooms at Oxford. There were no oak chairs indeed, but there were very comfortable seats, covered with yellow damask, and a sofa to match; and pictures of Bishops and great men who had belonged to the college were hung round the walls; but all had a dreary, deserted look, and I could not enter into the glee of our old *custode,* who seemed rather to rejoice in the fact that the priests had been sent away, and told that if they wanted to eat they must work. " Cavour," he said, " was not so much set against the priests as Ricasoli was known to be."

After going over the Church and the College the old man took us into the Crypt, which is the really interesting part of the building. The monuments of the Kings of Piedmont, from Victor Amadeus, with one or two exceptions, are placed round a circular vaulted chamber, and in the centre is the tomb of Charles Albert, who died in exile of a broken heart, after the loss of the battle of Novara, when he fought for the independence of Italy.

The old faded tricolours and banners presented to him, when for a few months, in 1848, Lombardy was free from the Austrian dominion, still hang upon it; and mixing with them is the bright tricolour left there by the National Guard of Naples, only as late as March, 1861. Behind are two marble slabs, inscribed with " the eternal gratitude" of the work-people of Turin—men and women— to their unhappy king, and placed on his tomb about four years after his death.* And it was at

* Inscriptions on the tomb of Carlo Alberto in the Superga.
REGI CARLO ALBERTO
prœmia virtutis et meritorum
æterna quotidianis precibus
a Deo flagitamus.
Depositus die xiv Octobris, 1849.

this tomb that Victor Emmanuel is said to have made a solemn vow to carry out the work which his father had begun, and complete the independence of Italy.

People may call it ambition,—possibly he is ambitious;—but that there is a true, deep love of his country as the foundation of the vow, and the motive for its performance, it is impossible to doubt. He has had heavy trials to discipline him. Within the outer crypt, where his father lies, is a square chamber, filled with the tiny sarcophagi of the royal children who have lived but a few months or days,—amongst them are three of the family of Victor Emmanuel; and still farther, within an inner chamber, where the shelves are made ready for the dead, as in the Christian Catacombs of Rome, rest the bodies of his mother, his wife, and his brother, who died in one year: two of them in one month. Simple marble slabs cover the space filled by each coffin, and the royal children are brought yearly to pray before their parents' tombs.

A Carlo Alberto che redenti i suoi popoli a nuova vita—Italia tutta voleva far libera—mille e mille socii operai riuniti, questo marmo simbolo di eterna riconoscenza il di 8 Agosto, 1852, consacravano.

Rè Carlo Alberto. Il tuo cenere muto ma glorioso convengono a lagrimare anche le buone del tuo popolo.
Le operaie di Torino
Il 11 Ottòbre, 1853.

They were at the Superga about a fortnight ago, and our old *custode* described them as dining in the College Hall, and playing about in the corridors, and then being taken down into the Crypt to say their prayers.

In this inner chamber the King wishes to have the body of Cavour placed—the only subject amongst the dead kings and princes. Whether it will be done is uncertain, for the Count's relations wish him to be laid with his own family. I should like myself to think that he was at the Superga; it would be such a proof of the King's feeling for him. Our *custode* spoke as if he knew Cavour well;— " He was so merry," he said, " and so kind and pleasant to every one: talking to all alike; and singing and laughing as if he had no care. He did everything for the King, who had no anxiety whilst Cavour was living; but now—'*ah! piangeva molto!*'"

This same character has been given of Count Cavour to-day by one of the Deputies, to whom we had a letter of introduction, and who brought us tickets for the Parliament, which were better than those of our Sicilian friend, as they gave admission to the gallery set apart for the diplomatic body. Speaking of Cavour, he said, " He was so good and kind to every one; it was an irreparable, universal loss!" The tears filled his eyes all the time we were talking of the Count; and then, as he said—and as is generally allowed—Cavour was wrongly treated by the Turin physicians!

Wednesday Morning. Como. Villa d'Este,—now the Hôtel de la Reine d'Angleterre.—I am sitting alone in my bedroom; the windows opening upon a stone balcony, the lake washing the walls of the house; the gardens of the Villa to the right;—in the distance, across the lake, Como and the hills which rise above it. Having told you so much, I shall go back to Turin and the Parliament.

We went between three and four, (for Italians do not hold their sittings as late as we do,) and had some difficulty in finding our way through the halls and staircases of the strange old Palace, which is now the Chamber of Deputies,—but we did at last reach the gallery of the Corps Diplomatique. The Chamber is handsome;—semicircular; the benches covered with crimson velvet, the desks in front green. There were about two hundred members present: grave, earnest, gentlemanly-looking men, with paper and writing materials before them; attendants in black, with tricoloured scarves round their arms, were moving about amongst them continually. The Ministers sat at a long table fronting the semicircle; the President, (Speaker, we should call him,) with the clerks, were on a raised dais behind them. The President was Ratazzi, who was

Prime Minister when Cavour retired after the Peace of Villafranca. An Italian gentleman who was in the gallery with us told us the names of some others: General Fanti, one of the Ministers, who took Perugia after the entrance of the Papal troops; Crespi, an ultra-liberal; Farini, Lanza, Poerio,—the Neapolitan who was so many years in exile—a pale, worn-looking man, with a face full of thought and quietness; and the Marquis de Cavour, the Count's brother, who sat alone, reading a paper, and left the House before we did. The discussion going on, it was impossible to follow, except once, when the Deputy who spoke was near us, so that we could catch his words. We learnt afterwards that it was an important one, though not what we should have been likely to understand easily. It referred to the funding and uniting of the debts of all the States which have given in their adhesion to Piedmont, so as to make them not the debts of separate provinces, but of the kingdom of Italy. Of course this is a grave matter, essential to the well-being and unity of the State. The President read some proposition, and then the Deputies discussed it, in short speeches, with a little action, but not as much as I expected. and in a very temperate tone. When all had said their say, hands were raised either to affirm or negative the proposition, and so they proceeded to the next. After all the propositions had been gone through, the Deputies left their seats, and passed singly before a table placed behind the Ministers, and on which stood two vases,—a white and a black one. The clerk called their names, (at least so I imagined,) and then each Deputy, as he went by, placed two balls, a black and a white one, in the vases. The balls in the white vase were counted, and those in the black thrown away, as having been merely used as a blind. When white balls predominate in the white vase, the question is carried. On this occasion there were only seven negatives.

All this would be common-place in England, but I cannot tell you the feeling it gives one in Italy; and now all is so intensely sad and earnest. Not only the prospects of the country, but the very existence of thousands, must depend upon the action of the Parliament. A little weakness, a few false steps,—and Austrian bayonets may be in Piedmont, and Poerio may again be in a Neapolitan dungeon. It is no child's game,—it is not even a human struggle of ambition which these men have undertaken; it is a contest for life or death. And those who may be inclined to think otherwise should pass, as we passed yesterday, over the battle-field of Magenta; and whilst looking at the white crosses in the deep ditch, by the side of the railway, marking where hundreds lie buried, should hear the day described by two Venetians—a gentleman and lady —returning to Venice after one month's leave of absence: all that could be obtained from the Austrian Government. Such bitter, bitter suffering they depicted, when speaking of their present condition; such a jarring laugh of all but despair was heard when they spoke of hope! It has haunted me ever since. Venice, they said, was a *tomb*. The best Italian families were ruined; their rents were not sufficient to pay the taxes imposed upon them, and they were obliged to borrow money that they might live. The Austrian soldiers thronged in every direction; they filled the villas in the country; there was no escape from them. Padua was being converted into a strong fortress; and, in fact, they were encircled by walls. The prison awaited all persons who dared to speak their minds freely; the young men were sent into exile; parents and children separated for years; and the innocent were continually arrested. Thirty thousand Venetians had, in the space of the last two years, left Venice for Piedmont; but no one could go now. Six months' leave was the very utmost term of absence that could ever be obtained. At the end of that time, if they did not return, their property would be confiscated. And then the Peace of Villafranca! the horrible disappointment, after seeing the French fleet before Venice;—waiting, day after day, expecting their deliverance,—and then to learn that their chains were more firmly riveted than ever! It made one's heart sick to hear them talk of it. But there was no bitterness against the Emperor or against any one. They were two quiet-mannered, moderate-speaking people,—such as one might meet any day; only with such an expression of deep suffering on their faces when they were led to talk of their country, as we, in England, cannot conceive. They were going back by the railway, travelling just as we might travel, with no apparent change of scenery or language to mark the line between freedom and oppression. One step made all the difference; but that one step must be taken, or they would be ruined.

And so it has been with Lombardy and Piedmont, and so it may be again. It is all one country. The distance between Milan and Turin is but two hours and a half; and when Carlo Alberto fought and lost the battle of Novara, which caused him to die the death of a heart-broken exile, he was but one hour from his capital. You will say I am full of Italy; but if you could come to Italy yourself, it would be impossible for you not to feel the same. Cavour's death grows worse and worse as a loss, and the grief meets one at every turn. The Italian flag, draped with black, is exhibited in little villages as in great towns. At Milan yesterday, the porch of the church opposite the hotel at which we stopped had a large black and white banner over it, with the inscription, "To Camillo Cavour—not funereal pomp, but the Christian offering of hearts which cannot forget."

This Lake of Como is inexpressibly lovely and peaceful; but somehow, the Italian world is sad.

Wednesday Evening.—The clock in the little Campanile, which I see from my window, is striking eight. I have just returned from a walk alone, through the grounds of a villa about five minutes' distance from the hotel. Everyone else was too tired to move. I wandered on through the path cut in the side of the hill which rises above the Lake, catching exquisite views of the water, and the points of land, the villas, and towns, and mountains, with a foreground of rock and cypresses, and at last I found a stone seat on the summit of a magnificent rock, descending abruptly to the Lake, on which I sat down to read and rest. I may have many such walks whilst I am here; it is too hot for excursions. The Lake in the cool evening, and the villas on its shores, are all we are likely to attempt.

Yours, &c. &c.

We were at Como for a week; it was a time of great repose. We went on the water nearly every evening. The villas are perfectly beautiful,—flowers in profusion, rocks, shrubs, trees, cliffs, mountains, cascades, and the blue lake; nothing is wanting, except—sometimes I thought of Rasselas in the happy valley, and felt it possible I might sigh for freedom.

We went up Monte Bisbino one day. It was a second edition of Palestrina, as regarded the donkeys, and the saddles, and the path; but it was a lovely and satisfying expedition, save only that the view from the summit was clouded, and instead of seeing Mont Blanc we only saw the Splugen at intervals, and the Resegone, which is almost historically interesting from the remembrance of the opening scene in the " Promessi Sposi."

My guide talked English, and had relations in England. We spoke of Italian politics, and Cavour's death, and Garibaldi's exploits, which were all performed in this neighbourhood. " The departure of the Austrians," he said, " was a great boon. Before, they could never go for a quarter of an hour's walk without being asked for a passport. He thought it would not be well to make an attempt upon Venetia yet; Rome must be gained first, and Naples consolidated." He was, in fact, as well-versed in the outline of politics as a parliamentary deputy; but these subjects are no speculations with Italians, they are a part of their daily life. Persons of all classes suffer, and therefore think.

Our last evening row upon the Lake was to the

Villa Pliniana, one of the most beautiful in our immediate neighbourhood. It might be a paradise of innocent delight, but it had a tale of sin and sorrow attached to it. Those who had last inhabited it broke the laws of God and man, and, escaping from Parisian fashionable life, thought to find happiness in the secluded beauty of a villa on the Lake of Como. But death had followed them, and now the large rooms, painted with such taste, are empty, and the handsome furniture is useless; and a gloom haunts the place, which even the charms of nature cannot dispel. The Villa Pliniana is not really Pliny's Villa, it is only so called because of an intermitting spring which he mentions as being discovered there. The house touches the Lake, and the walls of the garden are built up from the water's edge,—the roses clustering over them, so that they might be gathered whilst standing in a boat.

Excessively hot it was that evening, but the night was splendid with clouds and moonlight; and very hot it was too the next day, when we went up the Lake in the steamer, passing that most perfect part of it by Bellagio and the Villa Sommariva, where vines and flowers, terraces and trellis-work, lie at the foot of craggy mountains and snow-peaks. It was the last bit of real Italy. We landed at Colico and drove up the valley shut in by giant cliffs, which leads to Chiavenna, and there we once more looked upon vines, but they had lost their softening accompaniments of chestnuts and olive-groves, and the rocks and mountains were more Swiss than Italian.

We were on our way to Germany, by the Splugen, Coire, and the Lake of Constance. Langen Schwalbach was our ultimate destination. At another time the tour would have been pleasant in anticipation, and its termination far from disagreeable; but we had no heart then to look forward to it, for who has ever without a pang said farewell to Italy?

THE END.

www.ingramcontent.com/pod-product-compliance
Lightning Source LLC
Chambersburg PA
CBHW030002240426
43672CB00007B/791